Religion Enters the Academy

George H. Shriver
Lecture Series
in Religion
in American History
No. 4

Religion Enters the Academy

*The Origins of the Scholarly Study
of Religion in America*

JAMES TURNER

THE UNIVERSITY OF GEORGIA PRESS

Athens & London

Paperback edition, 2012

© 2011 by the University of Georgia Press

Athens, Georgia 30602

www.ugapress.org

All rights reserved

Designed by Walton Harris

Set in 11/15 Garamond Premiere Pro

Printed digitally in the United States of America

The Library of Congress has cataloged the hardcover
edition of this book as follows:

Turner, James, 1946–
Religion enters the academy : the origins of the scholarly study
of religion in America / James Turner.

p.   cm. — (George H. Shriver lecture series
in religion in American history ; no. 4)

Includes bibliographical references and index.

ISBN-13: 978-0-8203-3740-1 (hardcover : alk. paper)

ISBN-10: 0-8203-3740-4 (hardcover : alk. paper)

1. Religion—Study and teaching—United States—History—
19th century. 2. Religions—Study and teaching—United
States—History—19th century. I. Title.

BL41.T86 2010

200.07'073—dc22   2010026447

Paperback ISBN-13: 978-0-8203-4418-8

ISBN-10: 0-8203-4418-4

British Library Cataloging-in-Publication Data available

For Barb

CONTENTS

FOREWORD

The material in these chapters was originally presented as the 2010 George H. Shriver Lectures: Religion in American History at Stetson University, February 9–10, 2010. The Shriver Lectures were established by Dr. George Shriver, an alumnus of Stetson University and professor of history emeritus at Georgia Southern University. After receiving a bachelor of arts degree in both history and English at Stetson, Dr. Shriver later earned a doctor of philosophy degree in religious historical studies from Duke University. A noted scholar both in and out of the classroom, Dr. Shriver won several teaching awards during his career and is the author of numerous books and publications, including *Philip Schaff: Christian Scholar and Ecumenical Prophet* and *Contemporary Reflections on the Medieval Christian Tradition*. His endowment of these lectures, which also underwrites their publication, continues his lifetime commitment as scholar and educator.

The 2010 Shriver Lectures were delivered by Dr. James Turner, the Cavanaugh Professor of Humanities and professor of history at the University of Notre Dame, where he also teaches in the doctoral program in the History and Philosophy of Science. In addition to publishing numerous articles in international journals, he is the editor of one book and the author of six, including *The Sacred and the Secular University* (with Jon Roberts; Princeton University Press,

2000); *Language, Religion, Knowledge* (University of Notre Dame Press, 2003); and *The Future of Christian Learning* (with Mark A. Noll; Brazos Press, 2008).

Dr. Turner's three lectures examine the origins and growth of the academic study of religion in America. Beginning with western Europeans' and early Americans' almost total lack of attention to the religious beliefs and practices of other people, Turner traces their slowly awakening interest in non-European religions, an interest fueled more by religious purposes than by disinterested scholarship. Misinformed naiveté and prejudicial curiosity about other religions ultimately led in the late 1800s to the serious, scholarly study of religion, culminating in the establishment of religious studies as an accepted and respected discipline in American higher education. Appropriately for a lecture series delivered in 2010, the one-hundredth anniversary of the death of William James, Professor Turner in his last lecture in the series calls special attention to the contributions made by James's well-known work *The Varieties of Religious Experience* to the new discipline of the study of religion in the United States. With wit and insight, Turner's lectures provide a lively overview of an important aspect of American religious history and thus make a solid and fitting addition to the Shriver Lectures.

Stetson University deeply appreciates the generosity of George Shriver in his establishment of this lecture series. Through his own persistence and financial sacrifice, Dr. Shriver has made a lasting contribution to scholarship in religious studies and American history. Sincere thanks are also due to the following persons: James Turner, not only for the excellence of his lectures, but also for his graciousness during his visit; Paul Steeves, professor of history at Stetson University and member of the Shriver Lectures Committee, for his assistance in planning and implementing the lectures; Lisa Guenther, administrative specialist in the Department of Religious

Studies, for her usual careful attention to all the details surrounding the lectures; and the editors and staff of the University of Georgia Press for the publication of this series.

MITCHELL G. REDDISH, Chair
George H. Shriver Lectures Committee
Stetson University

PREFACE

This book began as the George H. Shriver Lectures on Religion in American History delivered at Stetson University in DeLand, Florida, in February 2010. The following pages perhaps retain some of the informality of their origin at the podium.

I am grateful to George Shriver for making the lectures possible and for the pleasure of his company during my time at Stetson. My thanks go likewise to my hosts there for their welcoming hospitality and smooth arrangement of the details of my visit. Professor Mitchell Reddish and Ms. Lisa Guenther of the Department of Religious Studies, in particular, made my few days at Stetson seem much too short. Professor Paul Croce of the American Studies Department generously shared his wise and learned views of William James. The reader should be as thankful as I am for the expert editing of the book by John Joerschke and the staff of the University of Georgia Press.

It may help readers to know that I am preparing a history of humanistic scholarship in the West from antiquity to the twentieth century, with a focus on the English-speaking North Atlantic countries after 1750. These lectures draw on some of my research for that book (as well as on a good deal of additional research). Work on this larger history has shaped my perspective on the birth of the particular humanistic discipline under scrutiny here.

Religion Enters the Academy

CHAPTER ONE

The Dog That Didn't Bark

The Study of Religions in America to circa 1820

No one would recoil in shock if, while scrolling through a university's Web site, she found a department of religious studies. The religion department routinely steps up to the plate in the batting order of the humanities today. The academic study of religion first appeared in American higher education during the same formative period as the other modern humanistic disciplines; that is, the latter half of the nineteenth century.[1] Religious studies got into the game a little later than history and literature but about the same time as art history and anthropology. (Cultural and social anthropology today usually get grouped with the social sciences. Intellectual ancestry and methods link these forms of anthropology more properly with the humanities.[2]) In origin the discipline of religious studies shared common roots and aims with the other humanities, and I suppose it still does. We argue a lot nowadays about just what the humanities do. But, whatever they do, no one is surprised to find religious studies doing it, too.

We *should* be. If you look earlier than the modern era to find inquirers in the West who took seriously the supernatural beliefs and rituals of other cultures, you have to go very far back — all the way back to polytheistic antiquity. The classic (so to speak) case is Herodotus's *History*, or *Histories*, written around 430 B.C.E. Herodotus tiptoed gingerly around Persian and Egyptian divinities (gods are best not toyed with), but he took them on their own terms, as he understood these, and managed to say quite a bit. Later, as Roman control gradually expanded across the Mediterranean world, the conquerors added a number of foreign deities to their own pantheon. Yet when Christian monotheism came to rule the West, from the fourth century C.E., polytheistic curiosity about other peoples' gods gave way to Christian hostility to them. 'Pagans,' 'infidels,' and 'heathens' became targets for conversion or eradication rather than for curiosity and inquiry.[3]

This about-face made a lot of sense. Polytheists accepted that their native deities were not the only mighty gods. Even in the earlier books of the Hebrew Bible, Yahweh competed with other Semitic deities. The ancient Israelites eventually turned into monotheists, who believed that only one god really existed. But for a polytheist, adding a new temple to those where you already worshipped could not hurt, might help. Strangers' gods at least bore looking into. The sore thumbs in the pagan Roman Empire were the Jews and later the Christians, who refused to adore any god but their own. Once Christian monotheists attained power over the state, they of course behaved much less flexibly than their polytheistic predecessors.

For Christians, only one God existed, and He got very upset when His people dallied with impostors. So insisted the first commandment, and for over a millennium the first commandment defined the place of other gods in Christian Europe, latterly in Christian America as well. "I am the Lord thy God. . . . Thou shalt have no other gods before me."[4] (The first commandment bound Jews as well as Christians, but in Christendom Jews were persecuted, not persecutors.) Non-Christian gods were false gods, and they got treated as false gods deserved. Christian scholars who took a more benign interest in non-Christian religions during the Middle Ages, such as Roger Bacon in the thirteenth century and Nicholas of Cusa in the fifteenth, stand out as real oddities, although neither came close to putting other religions on a par with Christianity. The wonder is that this bitter enmity eventually dissolved, and dissolved so completely that study of the various religions of the world now inhabits our college curricula.

How did this happen? As in other academic disciplines, scholars in religious studies have written its history, explaining its origins.[5] (Outside of higher education, tolerance crept in less dramatically but unmistakably.[6]) The tale usually starts at the end of the Middle Ages, with the expansion of Europe into Asia, Africa, and the Americas. Christians had long classified other peoples' faiths by contrasting Christian truth to Jewish perfidy and Muslim fraud. Europeans in the Age of Discovery sailed beyond this familiar triad. Explorers struggled to make sense of the strange beliefs and rites they encountered among peoples of newfound lands. Their striving spurred investigations of these novel versions of the supernatural, inquiries generally both unsystematic and unsympathetic.[7]

At the same time, the evolution of learning within Europe had its own momentum. Philological studies of ancient texts, including the Bible, sharpened critical skills and critical attitudes. By the seventeenth century scholars had begun to analyze Middle Eastern cults that neighbored the religion of the Hebrews — bookish curiosity possibly whetted by the new discoveries overseas. The evidence commonly came from the Hebrew Bible or Old Testament itself. (I shall refer to the books of the Bible originally written in biblical Hebrew or Aramaic as 'Hebrew Bible' or 'Old Testament' depending on whether Jewish or Christian scriptures were in question — in this book most often the latter.) Comparisons began; some erudite writers even suggested cross-fertilization between Israel and its neighbors. The English polymath John Selden, in *De diis Syriis* (*On Syrian Gods*, 1617), investigated the Semitic deities who vied with Yahweh in the Old Testament. A Cambridge scholar, John Spencer, in *De legibus Hebraeorum ritualibus et earum rationibus libri tres*

(*Three Books on the Ritual Laws of the Hebrews and Their Reasons*, 1685), learnedly argued that the religious practices of ancient Hebrews originated in those of peoples around them, notably the Egyptians. A much later Cambridge scholar, no less an authority than the great nineteenth-century Semiticist William Robertson Smith, argued that Spencer "laid the foundations of the science of Comparative Religion" — but, alas, "his work was not followed up."[8]

In the eighteenth century new categories for analyzing religions developed. One key tool was the modern idea of 'myth' as a traditional story that fell outside the black-and-white categories of fact and falsehood, as opposed to the older way of European thinking in which a story had to be either factually true, mistaken, or a deliberate lie. We owe the modern concept of myth most directly to the University of Göttingen philologists Christian Gottlob Heyne (1729–1812) and Johann Gottfried Eichhorn (1753–1827). Even more basic, the concept of 'religion' itself, as something apart from any particular religion, became commonplace. (See the discussion of deism below.)

Meanwhile, scholarly agents of empire continued to expand European knowledge of nonwestern religions, of their 'sacred' literatures, and of the languages needed to read them. Between 1755 and 1761 a French student of Middle Eastern languages with the fragrant name Abraham Hyacinthe Anquetil-Duperron wandered through India. After returning to Europe, he published in 1771 three volumes of selections from Zoroastrian writings under the title *Zend-Avesta, ouvrage de Zorastre* (*Zend-Avesta, Book of Zoroaster*). Europe thus first came to know sacred Parsi texts. The most celebrated such intellectual explorer was Sir William Jones, a British judge in Calcutta. He already bore the nickname Oriental Jones for his knowledge of Asian languages before he sailed to India. In Bengal in the 1780s Jones, aided by Indian pandits, learned Sanskrit. This encounter resulted in Jones's postulating what became known as the Indo-European family of languages, but Jones also compared the gods of India with those of ancient Greece and Rome. Jones and a few other erudite servants of the British East India Company worked with Indian scholars to begin opening to westerners sacred texts in Sanskrit.[9] (Need one add that the learned Indians did not get the credit?) Today, departments of religion study Christianity and Judaism along with other religions; but it is essential to understand that in the *origin* of the discipline previously unfamiliar religions, especially those of South and East Asia, provided the catalyst.

Thus, by the middle of the nineteenth century, Europeans had amassed a vast miscellany of information about non-European religions. More books began to appear trying to make sense of it. Vans Kennedy, an obscure East India Company employee versed in Sanskrit, published in 1831 *Researches into the Nature and Affinity of Ancient and Hindu Mythology*. A highly visible biblical scholar, Wilhelm de Wette, issued in 1827 *Die Religion, ihr Wesen und ihre Erscheinungsformen und ihren Einfluss auf das Leben* (*Religion: Its Nature, the Forms in Which It Appears, and Its Influence on Life*). Both Hegel and Schopenhauer made the history of religions do heavy lifting in their philosophizing.

Finally, a handful of pioneers then turned this trove of data into a new university-based discipline known variously as comparative religion, history of religions, or the science of religion. In 1873 a prominent Oxford scholar of Sanskrit, Friedrich Max Müller, published an *Introduction to the Science of Religion*, based on lectures he had given at the Royal Institution in London in 1870.[10] Müller's *Introduction* is often taken as the founding manifesto of religious studies, the first to lay down a method and program for the comparative study of religion — professedly academic, impartial, scientific, and at least protodisciplinary. In 1877 Cornelius Petrus Tiele, sometimes called the cofounder of the discipline, began teaching the history of religions at the University of Leiden.[11] Other great names followed: William Robertson Smith, Emile Durkheim, James G. Frazer, Jane Harrison . . .

Now, there is nothing wrong with this story, except that all the names are European. Americans do pop up from time to time in standard histories of the origin of the field. The one who most often steps in for a cameo role is James Freeman Clarke, a Boston Unitarian minister who published in 1871 a study called *Ten Great Religions*. The book proved immensely popular, going through numerous reprints and editions. But Americans appear as superfluous ornaments on a Eurocentric history. The late English scholar Eric J. Sharpe (1933–2000), in his history of religious studies, declared in a kindly, almost regretful tone, "[Americans] of the scholarly status of W. D. Whitney, James Freeman Clarke and George Foot Moore were the equals of their European counterparts, but nevertheless there was very little they could do to make a *distinctively American* contribution to the comparative study of religion" in its formative years. Poor things. Sharpe, though English by birth and much of his education and university career, earned his Ph.D. at Uppsala, taught briefly at Minnesota, and spent his last two decades as a professor in Australia. This cosmopolitan background makes his dismissive comment stand out all the more sharply. And even the young but already learned American Sydney Ahlstrom agreed in 1962 that "the chief impetus" for "the scholarly and scientific" study of religions even in America was "until 1900 chiefly European."[12]

I am content for the moment to leave hanging Sharpe's assertion that there was nothing distinctive about religious studies in America, but I do insist that the field had its own distinct American prehistory. Homebuilt concerns led up to the founding of religious studies as an academic discipline in America in the last decades of the nineteenth century. The discipline of religious studies in the United States was *not* a European import, but a native manufacture, even though it incorporated foreign as well as homemade parts. This book is devoted to recovering the specifically American background of the academic study of religion. Few of the facts I shall mention will surprise experts; but they will appear in a new perspective, for no one has previously told this story of American origins as a connected narrative.[13] And the story is in some respects peculiar.

The remainder of this chapter will explore American inquiries into non-European religions from the colonial period up to roughly 1820. The second chapter will carry the story into the late nineteenth century. The third will examine the founding of the discipline in American universities and end by considering William James's version of the subject in his famous *Varieties of Religious Experience* (1902). As so often, James took a strikingly original view — one that challenged the very conception of the discipline as American scholars had come to understand it.

But I get ahead of myself. We need some definitions to start. First, the shorthand word America refers to the United States and to the British colonies out of which it grew, with apologies to Canadians and Latin Americans. Second, I know better than to try to define the word "religion," which shuffles meanings faster than a politician on the stump. It is close to a commonplace in the field that 'religion' is a Western category, reflecting the monotheistic nature of Judaism, Christianity, and Islam; it does not map closely onto the phenomena that scholars of religions investigate in other parts of the world.[14] But I am going to use 'religion' anyway to identify ideas or practices called religion by the writers I discuss — even when the people they studied had no concept like religion. Third, I need a handy term to label collectively religions other than Christianity and Judaism. These two faiths held a virtual monopoly over religion in Europe in the period I shall be discussing, although certainly not confined to Europe, so I am going to call the *other* religions — not Christian, not Jewish — 'non-European religions.' The characters in my story were all Christians or Jews, at least by upbringing, and they mostly focused their gaze on these other, 'non-European' religions, strange to them. Islam, by the way, should not have been strange to colonial Americans. The British colonies in America had a substantial Islamic presence in the eighteenth century. But these Muslims were African slaves, overlooked by the writers we are about to meet.

Where and when do we first encounter American inquirers into non-European religions? The Spanish invaders of the New World showed great curiosity about the religions of the people they encountered, even if also confusion and contempt. Columbus himself quizzed some of the people he misnamed Indios about their supernatural beliefs.[15] The early British intruders in North America behaved quite differently. They had no choice but to deal with the indigenous population: European survival depended on the peoples whom the British also called Indians. Seventeenth-century British explorers, settlers, and missionaries occasionally commented on customs and lifestyles of native tribes. Yet the British rarely mentioned what we would call the natives' religious beliefs. Now, one might expect that missionaries dedicated to converting the Indians of North America to Christianity would pay a lot of attention to indigenous religion. After all, it might help you to persuade the Indians to spurn their heathen rites if you knew a little bit about those rites. But what strikes a reader today is how little even missionaries had to say about North American native religion, as opposed to, say, clothing or other material goods.

This reticence does have a plausible explanation. Iberians — both Spanish and Portuguese — had a lot of previous experience with non-European peoples and their religions. Iberians ran into newfound rites in the Canary Islands at the end of the Middle Ages; along the African coast during the fifteenth century as Prince Henry's navigators sought a sea route to the spices of the Indies; and in India itself when Vasco da Gama finally got there in 1498. Indeed,

Muslims had once ruled most of Iberia and were not completely driven from power until the year Columbus sailed.

Moreover, as Roman Catholics, Iberians inherited a Thomist intellectual tradition. Thomism made more room for non-European religions than the ways of thinking generally available to British Protestants. For Thomas Aquinas not only recognized a natural human propensity to worship (as Cicero had before him), but he also, in the *Summa contra gentiles*, argued that unaided human reason teaches the existence, unity, and goodness of God. Toward the end of the sixteenth century the Spanish historian Alonso de Espinosa (a Dominican like Aquinas) drew on Aquinas's thinking in arguing that the Guanche people native to the Canary Islands practiced a kind of natural religion. A hundred years earlier, Christopher Columbus articulated a cruder version of the same idea in describing the religion of the first native peoples he encountered in the New World.[16]

Iberians thus entered the New World 'prepped' to cope with unfamiliar religious beliefs and practices: their eyes wider open than those of Europeans to the north. Iberian lenses often produced badly distorted images. The Stone-Age Canarians' votive offerings of poured milk seem to have reminded Iberian observers of both Christian holy water and ancient Greek and Roman libations. The Portuguese who first saw Hindu gods painted on temple walls thought they were looking at Christian saints in a Christian church — though surely the extra arms must have puzzled them. Nor did Iberians see non-European rites as religion, properly speaking. Only Christianity qualified as legitimate religion; all else was error, perhaps illusion inspired by the devil. Thus Canarian or Mexican or Andean peoples could be seen as "seduced by demons."[17] But even such demonic delusions evidenced to Iberians a common human yearning for religion, and some of the invaders saw in local practices suggestive parallels to Christian rites. These could indicate openings for conversion to true religion instead of its demonic simulacrum.

But from the early British point of view, *North* American Indians had not even a facsimile of religion. These more provincial northern Europeans in the sixteenth and seventeenth centuries had at hand very limited categories for understanding the supernatural, whether religious or demonic: the three Mediterranean monotheistic faiths (Judaism, Christianity, Islam) plus ancient Mediterranean polytheism (Greek, Roman, Egyptian). The British had more recently heard rumors from parts of Asia and Spanish America; but it appears that the British in the New World had not processed this newer information enough to expand their mental frameworks. The supernatural systems of the native peoples who lived in what became the British North American colonies did not fit into any preexisting basket. (I avoid here saying North America in general. When Don Juan de Oñate and his companions marched into what is now New Mexico in 1598, they recognized the 'pueblo' Indians of this area as having a religion, though a diabolic one.) Not until the eighteenth century would a handful of English-speaking Americans begin to ask if the Indians had religion. Perhaps deists trumpeting the universality of 'natural religion' then inspired this novel way of thinking. Not until the nineteenth century would scholars elaborate concepts such as fetish and taboo into broad categories, however inadequate, for analyzing Indian religions.[18]

All this remained to come. Throughout the seventeenth century, offhand allusions to the devil — a familiar figure to English Protestants — sufficed to explain the Indians' relationship to the supernatural.[19] No parallels between Indian beliefs and real religion appeared to exist. Today one might see in this blindness haughty Europeans utterly dismissing Indian cultures. Not quite true.

Missionaries needed languages to communicate the Christian gospel, and so they did learn Indian *tongues*. So did traders with less elevated motives. Most of what we know about North American native languages in the colonial period we owe to manuscripts and a few printed texts by missionaries — admittedly, most of them French. Jacques Cartier's first voyage of Canadian exploration (1534) yielded a short Algonquian word list. When French missionaries moved into Canada in the 1610s, they quickly wrote down basic dictionaries of several Indian languages. These opened the floodgates for a wave of word lists, dictionaries, grammars, and similar aids that circulated in manuscript among the far-flung missionaries and occasionally found their way into print. By 1632 a "monograph-sized" dictionary of Huron and a catechism in that language had been published in the mother country. For many decades, French missionaries struggled to transliterate into Roman characters Ojibwa and Huron sounds never uttered by European tongues, sometimes concocting ingenious solutions.[20]

English missionaries to the south followed suit, though they were more flat-footed in approach and fewer in number. Yet however vigorous and wholehearted their grappling with native languages, the missionaries' efforts remained descriptive, particular, utilitarian. When taking ship for America, the English and French did not entirely leave behind a question animating contemporary European debates: what language did Adam and Eve speak in Paradise? So a few bookish types asked from which earlier tongue the Indians' 'corrupted' languages descended. Hebrew was the commonest answer.[21] But, as a rule, to classify, to compare, to theorize lay beyond the missionaries' horizon and their purposes. Still less did they try to understand the cultures expressed in the languages they studied.

And these English missionaries could hardly be expected to pay attention to religions that they could not really see, even in front of their faces. To them, converting an Indian to Christianity meant filling a vacuum rather than displacing a preexisting religion — or even a coherent demonic miming of religion. English Puritans regarded the Indians as blank slates on whose fresh, bare surfaces Christianity could be inscribed without the need to erase any pre-existing religion. Roger Williams proved a partial exception to this generalization, as to so many others, in dimly recognizing Indian polytheism. But even Williams looked on Indian deities as "Sathans Inventions."[22]

Interest in Indians did broaden a bit after 1700. Benjamin Franklin at least once seemed briefly alert to their creation myths — but deism shaped Franklin and, as we shall see in a moment, this mattered.[23] In the late eighteenth century, the study of Indian languages would take on a momentum of its own. This would lead in the nineteenth century to the scholarly study of Indian cultures, and these inquiries would finally open to Euroamerican eyes the varied religions of the North American Indians.[24] By 1900 these non-European religions would form a small, subordinate part of the new discipline of religious studies.

Yet almost all colonial Americans kept completely quiet about the non-European religions in their midst, and their silence typified the American response to any and all non-European religions before 1800: nearly utter disinterest. We hear the first faint whispers on the subject in New England in response to the English deist controversy of the earlier eighteenth century. Here the provocateurs were not heathen Indians who needed conversion but heretical Europeans who needed a dressing-down. Deism neither had nor has any consistent definition. But we get close enough for our purposes if we say that deists rejected the need for divine revelation, specifically the Bible. Instead, they believed people could learn all they needed to know for salvation from the evidences of divine purpose in nature. Potentially, such a conviction could inspire an inquirer to study the varied religions of humankind in order to discover beliefs shared by all clear-sighted human beings. Indeed, as Basil Willey long ago pointed out, "a pioneer-interest" in non-European religions encouraged Lord Herbert of Cherbury, the so-called father of deism, "to seek a common denominator for all religions" in the early seventeenth century.[25] Tenets believed everywhere would, ipso facto, add up to the basic universal religion, the religion of nature — however many frills people might add to it in the way of superfluous doctrines, silly rituals, and supposed revelations.

This idea did not spring full-blown from the brow of Lord Herbert. The roots of the concept of natural religion go deep into history, and deists were far from alone in appealing to it. In *De legibus*, widely read in early modern Europe, Cicero had already written that "there is no tribe, either civilized or savage, which does not know that it must recognize a god, even though it may not know what kind of god it should recognize."[26] This ancient concept of a natural *religiousness* points toward the idea of a natural *religion*; and Thomas Aquinas, as already mentioned, more or less arrived there. In short, the idea of natural religion flourished long before modern deism.

From the 1690s, Christian apologists wielded the idea as a weapon against the deists themselves — and against the threat of atheism they were perceived to represent. Anglican writers, in the so-called argument from design, claimed that the Creation showed the benevolent purposes of the Creator and thus pointed toward the plausibility of such a divine revelation as Christianity rested upon. Post-Newtonian Christian apologists such as Richard Bentley and John Ray loudly trumpeted this version of natural religion in the late seventeenth century in order to silence supposed atheists. Even their contemporary Samuel Willard, a Massachusetts Puritan, thought that "the curious contrivances" in nature illustrated the Creator's aims; and such notions became routine in America after 1700.[27] Such works, however, used natural religion only as a pointer to revealed Christianity, and they insisted on the subservience of reason to faith. Deists stood out not for believing in natural religion, but for believing in its sufficiency.

In the long run, the deist notion of natural religion set off a hunt for universal religious truths that supposedly underlay all religions of the world. This quest energized some of the pioneers of the discipline of religious studies — and would horrify most of their academic descendants today. In less metaphysical form, deist natural religion also eventually gave a new twist to the old idea that religion is natural to human beings: that religion, whatever its truth-value, satisfies some basic human need. Ergo, religion is a universal phenomenon. Religions crop up in virtually every culture, just as every culture evolves its own sexual customs or its own cuisine, developed around other basic human needs. This less ambitious conception of religion as 'natural' to human beings still implicitly grounds work in religious studies. Otherwise, one could not speak of 'religion' as a subject. Scholars in the discipline would be studying completely unrelated phenomena when they studied different religions, and there would be no point in drawing parallels or distinctions between them. In this sense, we owe academic religious studies to the deists. Every religion department should erect a little altar in the department chair's office to venerate its household gods: Lord Herbert of Cherbury, Thomas Chubb, Anthony Collins, Matthew Tindal, and the rest of the seventeenth- and eighteenth-century writers who gave us deism.[28]

Equipped with this information, we can begin gradually to move back toward the more immediate, American point. Deism as a self-conscious movement originated in England, its roots running back to the earlier seventeenth century. Many Christians then stood with daggers drawn, ready to cut each other's throats over disputed points of doctrine. In this context the appeal of a simple, universal, natural religion needs no explanation. But these very dangers encouraged the prudent heterodox to keep their heads down and mouths shut.

In the increasingly tolerant atmosphere of the 1690s, burning heretics fell out of fashion in England. Even the Scots, made of sterner stuff, reluctantly gave it up. In 1697 Edinburgh hanged a twenty-year-old student, Thomas Aikenhead, for outspoken blasphemy. (He seems to have been something of a Spinozist.)[29] Aikenhead turned out to be the last person executed anywhere in Britain for denying Christian beliefs. Deists crept cautiously out of the closet, keeping a weather eye on the magistrates and picking their words carefully. No deist writer was as careless in print as Aikenhead appears to have been in speech. But they did publish.

The deist controversy that then erupted — and did not die down until the late 1730s — spilled over the Atlantic.[30] Possibly a few colonists adopted deism at this time, but the young Benjamin Franklin stands out as not only the best known but the only one certainly known. For the rest of his life Franklin tacked and veered in religion, partly for prudential reasons, partly as his thinking changed. As a result debate will probably never cease about what he finally believed — though he certainly never embraced conventional Christianity.[31] Later, toward the end of the eighteenth century, deism would exercise far more influence in America, including swaying several of the Founders, but this later phase does not now concern us.[32] Instead we need to appreciate the strikingly divergent British and American responses to the deists' anti-Christian polemic.

Bashing Christianity was the stock in trade of deist writers, and from time to time they used comparisons with non-European religions as one of their sticks to beat it with. These weapons could be pretty crude. John Toland, who identified natural religion with pantheism, enlisted in his cause the "most ancient Egyptians, Persians, and Romans," along with "the first Patriarchs of the Hebrews" *and* the ancient Celtic druids. (Druids proved especially useful since in fact no one knew the slightest thing about their beliefs, making them a blank slate on which a writer could scribble anything he pleased.) A much more moderate writer, Arthur Bury, who perhaps teetered on the edge of deism but remained at least in principle a Christian, insisted in 1690 that the agreements between Islam and Christianity far outweighed their differences; indeed, "*Mahomet* professed all the articles of the Christian faith" — though only because he had stolen them. The restatement in "the *Alcoran*" of the truths in the Christian gospels, Bury went on, helps to explain the success of Islam. (Bury played by the accepted Christian rules in deriding "*Mahomet*" as a "lewd Impostor.") Matthew Tindal wrote *Christianity as Old as the Creation* (1730), sometimes called the Bible of deism. In it he compared the clear moral teachings of Confucius favorably with the confused ones of Jesus. "I am so far from thinking the Maxims of Confucius, and Jesus Christ to differ; that I think the plain and simple Maxims of the former, will help to illustrate the more obscures [sic] ones of the latter, accommodated to the then Way of speaking." Deists indeed grew particularly fond of Confucius, perhaps because he represented morality without the supernatural. Benjamin Franklin praised him and, in 1738, published excerpts from his writings in the *Pennsylvania Gazette*. In beating Christians about the head with non-European religions, deists may have encouraged the comparative investigation of religions, although disinterested scholarship was not their forte.[33]

But English deists were not alone in using comparisons with other religions as a club in this brawl. Some of their Anglican foes replied in kind. The Reverend William Warburton's *Divine Legation of Moses* (1738–41) aimed to vindicate the supernatural origin of the Mosaic dispensation against unbelievers like Tindal. In the course of defending the ancient Hebrews' close personal relationship with the deity, Warburton tossed off an astonishing farrago of information about the ancient world. He mused on everything from mystery cults to the origin of language. Among many other things, he advanced earlier comparative researches into the origin of Hebraic rituals in resistance to parallel Egyptian ones. Another Anglican parson, Conyers Middleton, whose loyalty to Christianity was more ambiguous than Warburton's, likewise reckoned that the ancient Hebrews must have adopted some of their rites from the Egyptians — though in his case because primitive Israelites had to borrow from their sophisticated Egyptian superiors. But by Warburton and Middleton's day, Thomas Blackwell, a Scottish scholar who did not even have a dog in the fight over deism, could blithely compare the creation story in Genesis with Phoenician tales. In short, before the middle of the eighteenth century, comparing the biblical religions with other rites had become something of a parlor game in the United Kingdom — one outpost of a widespread European fascination with nonbiblical religions during the eighteenth century.[34]

Here American writers stood out like kindergarteners in college. Even Americans who kept up with contemporary British intellectual life showed vanishingly little interest in comparing religions. Deist snickering at Christianity did inspire retorts from a few American ministers in the first decades of the eighteenth century, but without notice of non-European religions. The virtual absence of deists in his America did not stop the Reverend Cotton Mather of Boston (1663–1728), who put pen to paper at the slightest provocation, from leaping into the fray. Yet the polymathic Mather, curious about almost everything, showed no curiosity at all about the non-European religions that deists touted. His very few offhand references even to Islam — a conventional whipping-boy for Christian apologists — only mentioned Muslims in order to denounce deists as still worse. (In a similar vein, Mather cited supposed travelers' reports of "*whole Sermons* on the Glories of a JESUS" in "*Mohametan Moschs* [mosques]" to shame Christian preachers who failed to live up to Mather's Christocentrism.) Mather's neglect is all the odder considering that he actually owned a copy of the Qur'an. And he did have a strong interest in South Asia and the Ottoman Empire and read a good deal about both areas. But he ignored the religions of these parts of the world. His disinterest made him entirely typical of eighteenth-century Americans. Their rare allusions to non-European religions simply repeated traditional, abstract censure of treacherous Muslims and benighted heathens.[35]

Apparently the one real exception to this generalization prior to the American Revolution, besides possibly Benjamin Franklin, was Franklin's antitype, the brilliant defender of orthodox Calvinism Jonathan Edwards (1703–58).[36] We do have tantalizing hints that one or two others may have taken a brief, passing interest in non-European religions. For instance, in 1733 James Logan of Philadelphia was curious enough to purchase a copy of the first European printing of Confucius's writings.[37] But Edwards alone grappled seriously with the deist assault on Christian particularity. Here is the problem Edwards faced: Was it plausible, deists asked, to believe that God first revealed the means of salvation to one small tribe in a backwards corner of West Asia and then spread it only to Christians, leaving the rest of humankind to roast in hell? Would not a just God have revealed saving truth to all peoples? Solving this dilemma required some wrestling with non-European religions, and Edwards in his private notebooks tried to face up to the challenge. In doing so, he drew on scant, often unreliable reports in European books available to him; so his researches were unimpressive even by eighteenth-century standards. He was, for instance, badly misled as to the nature of Chinese religious or, better, philosophical thought. In most respects, Edwards remained very much an American of his times, contemptuous of Islam and dismissive of Native American religions as Satanic. But he viewed Chinese traditions and Greco-Roman polytheists more favorably.

Edwards believed that these peoples had preserved bits and pieces of true revelation, which foreshadowed Christianity. Noah and his sons, or maybe the ancient Hebrews, had passed along the information. In proposing this theory, Edwards articulated an old notion, found already in St. Augustine, that a so-called *prisca theologia* — ancient theology — survived in distorted form in some pre-Christian faiths. The idea had already grown historically very implausible by Edwards's day. But *prisca theologia* — combined perhaps with the increasingly distinct idea of 'religion' as a general phenomenon — enabled him to see at least some non-European religions as real religions, worth comparing to Christianity, if only to learn how many shards of truth did sparkle among the dross. Yet Edwards's explorations were every bit as instrumental as the English deists', though serving opposite ends. And he published not a word of them.

American silence about non-European religions persisted into the heyday of the American Enlightenment in the late eighteenth century. This strikes us as all the odder because Enlightenment was famously nosy about other cultures. Compelling new theories of human social and cultural development were coming especially out of Enlightened Scotland — a country with which British North America had close intellectual ties. This Enlightened interest in human beings of other times or places took its best-known form in the Scottish invention of what eventually came to be called conjectural history. (Dugald Stewart, one of these Scots, belatedly invented this much needed label in 1795.[38]) Conjectural history aimed to discover general principles of the human mind by investigating the development of human cultures over time, including their religious practices. Scottish writers such as Adam Ferguson, Lord Kames, and Adam Smith argued that all human societies developed through similar stages of increasingly complex social organization. The analyst could — conjecturally — trace the progressive advance of the human mind through such phases. The stumbling block was that not even the most learned Scot knew the first thing about what we now call prehistoric peoples. (Prehistoric archaeology and anthropology took shape only in the mid-nineteenth century.) So conjectural history speculated about the long-ago past by using information about human societies that people *did* know something about, especially non-European ones.

This approach exerted potent influence in the infant United States.[39] One reason stands out. Conjectural history dovetailed with rising American theoretical interest in American Indians — rising, not coincidentally, even as real Indians were pushed out of the main areas of Euroamerican habitation. Native Americans also conveniently served Scottish conjectural historians as Exhibit A of Savage Man, a surrogate for the actual early human beings who had vanished into an unrecoverable past. The crucial publications of Ferguson, Kames, and Smith roughly coincided with the struggle of the American mainland colonies for independence from Britain; their books appeared, that is, at a time when Americans started to think of themselves as a distinct people. In this time of ferment, the character of the American Indians became attached to sensitive issues of American nationality, virility, amour-propre. Thomas Jefferson, for one, was famously concerned to refute the Comte de Buffon's libel that animals, including human ones, had degenerated in the New World: that the indigenous Americans, in particular, were cowardly, stupid, and undersexed. In this context serious studies of Indian language began in the United States — calculated no longer to aid missionaries, but to probe the origin of the original Americans. "A knowledge of their several languages would be," Jefferson wrote, "the most certain evidence of their derivation which could be produced."[40] Enlightened Americans *ought* to have longed for similar knowledge of Indian religions — what better testimony to their character? For that matter, simply as

Enlightened inquirers, Jefferson and his like *ought* to have hungered to know of the religions of any and every non-European culture.

They utterly failed to live up to our expectations. The Reverend William Bentley (1759–1819) of Salem, Massachusetts, was an archetypal Enlightenment man. His endless curiosity resulted in a huge private library, second in America only to Jefferson's in size and second to no one's in range. In collecting, Bentley benefited from Salem's position as a major port in the new, postrevolutionary American trade with India, China, and the Baltic. His books ran "from mineralogy to physiology, from Arabian literature to American law, from the theory of music to the art of navigation." He owned books by the English deists who had broached inquiry into non-European religions, along with some "Hindu and Muslim religious works in their original languages and in translation" and "studies of pagan cults," including Bergier's *Origine des dieux du paganisme* and Dupuis' *Origin of the Cults*. These titles have been taken as proving Bentley's "interest in comparative religion." But owning a book does not imply reading it, especially for a bibliomaniac like Bentley. Let us turn instead to Bentley's massive diary. The 2,077 pages of its four printed volumes never refer to Hinduism, Islam, Confucianism, or any other identifiable non-European religion. The diary's sole entry about non-European religions is a single, brief mention of a sea-captain's report of a "religious prohibition of killing animals" among some "extremely ignorant" denizens of present-day Myanmar, who may or may not have been Buddhists.[41] So much for Bentley's "interest in comparative religion." The letters written by that other bibliophile and universal man of the American Enlightenment, Thomas Jefferson, are equally devoid of substantive discussion of non-European religions.[42] John Adams wrote almost as little (unless one counts marginal scribblings in his books), although in old age he did *read* a good deal about the subject.[43]

By that time one major figure of the American Enlightenment had actually written a book about non-European religions. This precedent-breaker was the natural philosopher and Unitarian theologian Joseph Priestley. In 1794 Priestley abandoned England, where his radical politics had gotten him into hot water. At the age of sixty-one he settled in inland Pennsylvania. In 1799 he published there *A Comparison of the Institutions of Moses with Those of the Hindoos and Other Ancient Nations.*[44] (Tellingly, Jefferson was a friend of Priestley's, had a copy of this book from the author, but never mentioned it in his surviving letters.) Priestley had earlier written brief comparisons of "revealed religion" (that is, Judaism and Christianity) with classical paganism and with Islam.[45] But his 1799 book stretched over 450 pages and contained long, though flawed, expositions of the Vedas, the caste system, Hindu gods and myths, rituals, dietary restrictions, the position of women, and a host of other matters. He also included a briefer account of ancient Egyptian religion to refute the idea that Moses had borrowed from it; and he discussed Siberian shamanism, which he thought perhaps ancestral to Hinduism.[46] (As this last hypothesis suggests, Priestley entertained a very confused idea of what "Schamans" believed and did.) Priestley's purpose was apologetic, and he took special care to cite Hindu echoes of Jewish and Christian beliefs. He sought thus to prove the universality of the truths of the Old and New Testaments — universal truth from which Hindus had, in his view, sadly declined. It therefore does not surprise that "the Institutions of Moses" came out a lot better than "Those of the Hindoos." Priestley, indeed, could be pretty savage on the Hindus. But he had produced the first extended inquiry into a non-European religion published in the United States. Yet his book was the exception that proved the rule that Americans did not care about non-European religions. It took an English refugee to write the thing. Another expatriated Englishman, Thomas Paine, from time to time used

Confucianism as a club to bludgeon Christianity, in the standard deist style, though he never seriously investigated it.[47]

Why even late eighteenth-century Americans ignored non-European religions remains a puzzle. My stab in the dark — and it is no more than that — is that their apathy had something to do with the specific mode of Enlightenment that dominated American intellectual life. Most Americans who published books and articles fell under the sway of the relatively conservative, Scottish, 'common-sense' school of thought — what Henry May many years ago labeled 'the moderate Enlightenment.'[48] It was exemplified in the writings of the Reverend John Witherspoon, the Scot who came to America as president of the College of New Jersey (later Princeton University) and who remained to become a signer of the Declaration of Independence. Calvinism tinged this version of Enlightenment, and it strove to defend Christianity — the liveliest current foes of which were radical Enlightenment thinkers like the deists. The study of non-European religions was linked to the deist attack on Christianity. So looking into such religions may have seemed to the moderately Enlightened trafficking in the business of the enemy.

Still, conditions in the young United States were moving — economically, religiously, intellectually. These changes made the cultural environment gradually more encouraging of curiosity about non-European religions. Economically, a burgeoning trade with India and China brought more Americans into contact with Asia and its religions. In 1817, for example, a New England sailor named Amasa Delano published a narrative of his voyages. The book told about being bitten by a centipede and about earthquakes in Peru, and it also told a little about various religions of East and South Asia — not always accurate tales, to be sure, but capturing attention. (Herman Melville's "Benito Cereno" was based on an episode in Delano's *Narrative*.)[49]

Religiously, American missionary efforts to Asia began shortly after 1800, turning the attention of millions of evangelical Protestants to that part of the world. The 'haystack prayer meeting' of 1806, where a few Williams College students dedicated themselves to converting the heathen in foreign lands, is celebrated in lore. More substantially, New England Congregationalist ministers in 1810 founded the American Board of Commissioners for Foreign Missions. Baptists followed suit in 1814.

Intellectually, more resources appeared to support the study of non-European religions. British hegemony in India produced scholarly side effects; and from the 1790s onward, readers in the English-speaking world could find increasingly accurate descriptions of Hinduism and, eventually, of Buddhism, as well as more and more English translations of sacred texts. Publications of early British orientalists probably loosely informed Samuel Lorenzo Knapp's anonymous 1802 fiction *Letters of Shahcoolen, a Hindu Philosopher, Residing in Philadelphia; to his Friend El Hassan, an Inhabitant of Delhi*, a vehicle for ridiculing western ideas and mores of which Knapp disapproved, in the tradition of Montesquieu's *Lettres persanes*. Americans who read French, as many educated ones did, also had access to productions of the Paris school of oriental studies. By the 1820s, readers could find, too, a substantial number of books on China in American libraries. These included a general survey of Chinese history and culture published in 1823–24 by an American, Robert Waln Jr.; it devoted considerable attention to Chinese religion, although mostly to denigrate it.[50]

Priestley had taken advantage of the earliest of such textual resources, but the first native-born American to benefit much from them was Hannah Adams (1755–1831). Adams was apparently the first American woman to support herself with her pen[51], and her brief autobiography remains compelling reading. But for our purposes her writings on religion are what matter. They mark the shift from almost complete disinterest in non-European religions in the United States to serious engagement with them from the 1820s onward.[52]

To understand Adams, we need to recall the theological polemics that roiled her home state, Massachusetts, during her lifetime. These quarrels eventually split the Congregationalist establishment into opposing Unitarian and Trinitarian denominations. The argument was not carried on with kindly spirit and mild words. This theological bitterness decisively affected Adams.

The daughter of a bookish and incompetent shopkeeper, young Hannah suffered both ill health and poverty. In fact, the whole family seems to have tottered about in weak health, if not hypochondria. Hannah's poor health kept her out of school, and so she got to read voraciously. The poverty required her family to take in boarders, who exposed her, she said, to "the rudiments of Latin, Greek, geography, and logic." One of these informal teachers carried "a small manuscript" excerpted from a 1742 book titled *An Historical Dictionary of All Religions from the Creation of the World to This Present Time*.[53] This ambitious work, in two hefty volumes, had been written by an Anglican minister named Thomas Broughton. Broughton aimed "to give the reader a comprehensive view of the *principal matters* relating to the state of RELIGION, in all ages, and nations, of the known world." And he did cover a lot of ground, ranging from minor Roman deities to "LINGON" (presumably lingam), described by Broughton as "an Idol, worshipped by the Pagans of *Indostan*" and a "very leud [sic] figure."[54] Broughton's book aggressively insisted on the utter falsity of all religions except Christianity and its Hebrew antecedents; otherwise, it did not stand out from the several other works published by eighteenth-century Europeans to compare religions. But typically of eighteenth-century Americans, the Adams family boarder who copied from Broughton passed over all the non-European religions to write down a little extract relevant to the local Christian controversies then raging in New England.[55]

This meager excerpt somehow lit a fire in Hannah Adams. She plunged into the study of religion, "perusing all the books which I could obtain"—soon including Broughton—and transcribing her notes into a blank book. Adams was herself a Liberal Congregationalist; that is, a proto-Unitarian. But she had heard enough theological venom. She grew "disgusted" with the unrestrained biases of the authors she read. And as she began to think of printing her compilation—"induced" to publish by "poverty, not ambition, or vanity"—she strove to rise above prejudice and reproduce "what appeared to me the most plausible arguments" for each religious viewpoint.[56]

In 1784, almost a decade after she began taking notes, she published *An Alphabetical Compendium of the Various Sects Which Have Appeared in the World from the Beginning of the Christian Æra to the Present Day*, extending across 314 pages.[57] In 1791 a new version appeared, a hundred pages longer, under the title *A View of Religions*.[58] A third, still larger edition came out in 1801.[59] The title became, in the final version in 1817, *A Dictionary of All Religions and Religious Denominations, Jewish, Heathen, Mahometan, and Christian, Ancient and Modern*.[60] As these new editions unfolded, it was key that Adams eventually gained access both to the substantial private library of the Reverend Joseph Buckminster and to the Boston Athenæum, then one of the largest book collections in the United States.[61] Meanwhile, she was also writing a school history of New England, a history of the Jews, a defense of Christianity, and other works to keep her pots boiling.

The progression through the several versions of her *Alphabetical Compendium* and its successors tells us something about the changing awareness of—and attitudes toward—religions in Adams's country. Initially, to judge from both form and content of the first edition and from her own background, Adams meant to produce simply a compendium of Christian disputes. She set out to catalog meticulously every Christian subgroup she could locate. The main body of her *Alphabetical Compendium* thus dealt exclusively with Christians, ranging from obscure ancient heresies to the major denominations and fringe cults of her own day. She set herself a standard of disinterested objectivity that she had rarely seen in New England's wars of religion. She meant "to avoid giving the least preference of one denomination above another" and "to take the utmost care not to misrepresent the ideas." How well she fulfilled her aim is, to be sure, another question. Adams stumbled pretty badly when she came to the Jesuits, and she alphabetized Roman Catholics under P for Papists. At some point she decided to tack on to her encyclopedia of Christianity an appendix discussing non-Christian religions. Including Judaism and non-European religions in her book seems obviously an afterthought, and Adams put much less effort into tracking down details about these faiths. Yet even in discussing Islam, long a *bête noire* of Christians, she maintained flat affect. She simply reported — with nary a word of praise nor denigration.[62]

Yet it is a mistake to take Adams as a serious precursor of modern religious studies, as some historians have done.[63] Divisions among Christians sparked her interest, not the variety of religions in the world. All *other* religions — and she did call them religions — were relegated to eighty-four pages. She divided all non-Christian religions into four groups: "*Pagans, Mahometans, Jews* and *Deists*." In this appendix her relative sure-footedness in discussing Christian doctrine deserted her. This was likely a result of the quality of sources readily available to her in the early 1780s, as well as her lack of interest in searching for better ones. Not surprisingly she managed Judaism fairly well. She thought the most widespread "mode of *Paganism*" to be "worship" of the Dalai Lama, whom she imagined as a sort of pagan pope, exercising religious sway over China and India from his palace among "the *Thibetian Tartars.*" Her account of the religions of India was wildly distorted. She also got pretty confused in discussing Confucianism, by now tolerably well known in Europe. She stood on somewhat more solid ground in her more extensive summary of Islamic beliefs — with which, of course, European scholars had much longer familiarity. But she bizarrely believed most Filipinos to be Muslim. Still, in contrast to most earlier Euroamericans, Adams had no trouble recognizing something properly called religion in Native American cultures and in Siberian shamanism — although in the latter case perhaps because she so badly misunderstood shamanism that her version of it resembled deism. Yet so far had she reversed earlier American attitudes toward Native American religions that she found it extraordinary that "several tribes have been discovered" in Brazil "which have no idea whatever of a Supreme Being, and no rites of religious worship."[64]

Without exaggerating Adams's modernity and without ignoring the depth of her ignorance of non-European religions, the 1784 *Alphabetical Compendium* did stand out as the first American attempt to survey religions throughout the world. Moreover, Adams did recognize religion as a worldwide phenomenon, and she tried to take all religions seriously.

The second version of the work reorganized the material under the new title *A View of Religions, in Two Parts.* The alphabetical listing of Christian groups became part 1, and the appendix dealing mostly with non-Christian religions was elevated to a parallel part 2 and expanded from 80-some pages to over 130. The updating introduced some new materials but little increase in accuracy. For instance, Adams added a description by "an American traveller" of Chinese worship in a "joss house" — unrecognized by either the traveler or Adams as a Buddhist temple. (The traveler was Samuel

Shaw, supercargo on the first U.S. merchantman to call in China.) Adams was just catching sight of emerging British scholarship on Indian culture. She quoted Nathaniel Brassey Halhed's 1776 *Code of Gentoo Laws* but seemed unaware of Charles Wilkins's 1785 translation of the Bhagavad Gītā or the still more recent publications of the Asiatic Society of Bengal.[65]

The 1801 edition shows Adams's reading habits as getting a little closer to what might be regarded as scholarly, perhaps a result of better access to libraries, but only a little. She had, for example, learned how to spell 'Vedas' and found out that they were written in Sanskrit. She also quotes the *Researches* of the Asiatic Society of Bengal. She still lacked any real understanding of this particular scholarly world — witness her confused and exaggerated account of Sir William Jones's role in bringing Sanskrit "to light" after it had long "been concealed in the hands of the Bramins." She had also uncovered, unfortunately, Thomas Maurice's seven-volume popularization of Jones's researches. Maurice offered much information about Hindu India at the cost of warping it to fit a Christian triumphalism — perhaps part of his appeal to Adams. (Maurice may have shouted the last hurrah of *prisca theologia*.) The sum result was that Adams's account of Hinduism grew longer, a bit closer to reality, but even more Christocentric. By and large, her sources for non-European religions remained antiquated by the standards of European scholars of her day, even though her coverage of the subject had expanded to almost two hundred pages. The 1801 edition also went a little further to fit Christianity into a broader religious context. Adams provided background to the dictionary-style list of Christian sects (part 1) by prefacing it with a long, three-section introduction. This surveyed the religious state of the world — the immediately relevant world — at the time of Christ's birth: summarizing, first, pagan religious practices; second, divisions among the Jews; and, third, prevailing classical philosophical systems: all background to her steady focus on Christianity. Fundamentally, Adams remained fixated on divisions within Christianity.[66]

The 1817 edition made little scholarly advance on that of sixteen years previous, but it did sport a new title and a new arrangement. The *Dictionary of All Religions and Religious Denominations* now integrated material on Christian groups and non-Christian religions into a single alphabetically ordered encyclopedia. In short, all religions now stood, structurally at least, on the same footing. This innovation, however, was not Adams's brainchild. An Englishman named Thomas Williams had, two years earlier, taken her *View of Religions*, added new material to it, recast the whole in a single alphabetical sequence, and published the result in London. He titled his work *A Dictionary of All Religions*. Williams acknowledged Adams's authorship. In the absence of international copyright, even this was an act of generosity. Adams in turn adopted Williams's title and format and used some of his additions in her final 1817 American edition.[67] An English refugee, Priestley, had written the first substantial study of a non-European religion published in the United States. Now an English editor exported to America the idea that a disinterested study of religions should treat them with at least formal equality. The best we can say about Adams is that she liked this new notion enough to adopt it.

No one can say for sure why Hannah Adams decided to add non-European religions to her *Alphabetical Compendium*. Like most of her fellow Unitarians, she took a strongly historical approach to her real interest, Christianity. The true history of Christianity, in her view, was a narrative of progress toward its greatest perfection in Unitarianism. Given this understanding of religious evolution, my guess is that Adams wanted to situate the chronicle of Christian progress in the broadest possible context. But whatever her motive, her afterthought chimed with the beginnings of American interest in non-European religions, and she found with the second edition that she had a profit-maker on her hands.

Thus, as her book went through its samsara-like incarnations, it foreshadowed a broader change to come in the United States, a shift from ignoring non-European religions to treating them as worthy of understanding. But to class Adams as a "prophet and pioneer" of the academic discipline of religious studies, as Louis Henry Jordan did, is seriously to overestimate her competence and to underestimate the extent to which the internal quarrels of Christianity motivated her.[68]

Hannah Adams, to repeat, was a Unitarian. This turns out to be an interesting fact. Why will become apparent in the next chapter, which explores the foundations of real American scholarship on religions.

Comparing Religions in an Age of Uncertainty, circa 1820 to 1875

By the 1820s Americans had accessible many more particulars about non-European religions; they also then discovered specifically Christian reasons to care about them, going beyond generalized Enlightenment curiosity about other cultures. Broadly speaking, an unpredictable new factor — unpredictable when Hannah Adams first published — led eventually to the creation in America of an academic discipline dedicated to studying all religions. This wild card was the self-conscious development in the United States (as elsewhere) of an increasingly liberal version of Protestant theology. This heterodox theology provided the matrix for a surge of interest in those non-European religions that shared with Christianity both a wide geographic reach and a basis in normative texts.

I immediately add that hospitality toward non-European religions was far from common among American Protestants. More typical without question was James Moffat, professor of biblical criticism and literature in the Presbyterians' Cincinnati Theological Seminary. Moffat roundly declared in 1852, "The various shades of philanthropy may be traced from nation to nation, by the corresponding degrees of Christian knowledge. From the midnight blackness of Hindooism, through Mohammedanism, and Romanism, and formal Protestantism, to the humble, intelligent and faithful follower of the Word of God, you may distinctly grade the ascending scale of humanity."[1] Such aversion should not surprise. Most American Protestants got their pictures of the religions of Asia from reports sent home by missionaries trying to convert the heathen, and nineteenth-century American missionaries pretty consistently damned the 'abhorrent' religious practices of the people they were trying to turn into Christians.[2]

So the few surveys of non-European religions prepared by traditional Protestants before the late nineteenth century combined a stew of dubious 'facts' with a whopping side dish of distaste. Consider a book titled *All Religions and Religious Ceremonies*, published in Hartford in 1823. Part 1 of this mishmash offered a survey of Christian groups — tolerably fair-minded and disinterested, in the spirit of Hannah Adams — cribbed from various similar British encyclopedias (including Thomas Williams's edition of Adams). It also tried to treat Judaism objectively while sneering at Islam. Part 2 abridged the four-volume *Account of the Writings, Religion, and Manners of the Hindoos* (1811) by the English Baptist missionary William Ward (1766–1826). Ward uttered a few kind words about Indian legal and philological scholarship but savagely laid into Hindu "idolatry" and "superstition." Another Hartford printer published a stand-alone abridgment of Ward's book the following year. This suggests some popular demand for information about India and its religions. Similar in tone to Ward was the prolific Reverend Charles Goodrich's much reprinted *Pictorial and Descriptive View of All Religions* (1842). Goodrich cribbed his book from an English abridgment of a major Enlightenment work, Bernard Picart's *Cérémonies et coutumes religieuses de tous les peuples du monde* (*Ceremonies and Religious Customs of All Peoples of the World*, 1723–43). But Goodrich 'improved' Picart by adding proofs of the ongoing conquest of "idolatry" in "every portion of the globe" by the "crucified Redeemer." Meanwhile, the supposedly shrinking non-Christian religions offered Christians disgusting exhibits of "human degeneracy" (guaranteed to "furnish no small entertainment" to Goodrich's readers). Books like these seemed calculated to feed a morbid interest in the bizarre and frightful rather than to explore non-European religions seriously.[3]

A strikingly different attitude first appeared in the most liberal wing of American Protestantism, Unitarianism. Some wag defined the three essential dogmas of early nineteenth-century Unitarianism as the Fatherhood of God, the Brotherhood of Man, and the Neighborhood of Boston. The joke hit the mark. American Unitarianism hatched under the Liberal wing of New England Congregationalism between about 1800 and 1820, and for some decades it remained concentrated in eastern Massachusetts. This location matters for our purposes because America's new East India trade came to center in Boston. In 1807 Boston's iconic Federal-period architect, Charles Bulfinch, designed India Wharf to house the merchants and their cargos of hides, linseed, shellac, gunny bags, indigo, and jute. Most of the traders who populated India Wharf worshiped in Unitarian churches. For this reason, Unitarians tended to be far better acquainted with India than other Americans and far more interested in it. Indeed, the *Monthly Anthology*, which from 1803 to 1811 served as something like the house organ of Boston's Unitarian elite, several times called attention to the importance of Sir William Jones's Sanskrit researches, reprinted part of Jones's translation of Kālidāsa's greatest play, *Śakuntalā*, and in 1805 offered a long review of Lord Teignmouth's biography of Jones.[4]

With India looming over Boston harbor, it makes sense that in the 1820s Unitarians grew fascinated by a Westernized, English-speaking Hindu religious reformer named Rammohan Roy (1772?-1833). Rammohan believed Hindu polytheism to be a corruption of an originally monotheistic Indian religion. He urged Hindus to dump their multiple gods and 'return' to worshiping only one. His fellow Indians mostly ignored his pleas, but Rammohan made a splash in the West. He interpreted Christianity as he did Hinduism, rejecting what he saw as the 'polytheistic' doctrine of the Trinity. Predictably, Unitarians loved "this great man, patriot and philanthropist," as the 'Unitarian pope' Andrews Norton called him. Some Unitarians even took Rammohan *really* to be one of themselves.[5]

Let us pause to notice something significant. The Unitarians took Rammohan's version of Hinduism seriously *as a real religion.* Granted, they did so because of perceived affinity with Christianity. But they did not gaze at Rammohan's Hinduism through an ethnographic lens. As we have seen, Americans had shown little interest in the Enlightenment way of studying non-European religions as cultural artifacts or evidences. Perhaps because Americans now started with a nearly blank slate in their conception of non-European religions, these Unitarians did not try to fit Hinduism within something like the Scottish Enlightenment's progress-of-civilization framework. Instead — unselfconsciously as far as I can tell — they simply regarded Hinduism, at least Rammohan's Hinduism, as a religion parallel to their own and fit to be compared with their own.

Throughout the 1820s, Rammohan's name popped up repeatedly in Unitarian magazines — and from there radiated out into the broader American religious press, usually swathed in a positive glow. The publicity must have left many readers wondering about the ancient texts that Rammohan discussed, and he helped to satisfy their curiosity by translating selections from the Vedas and Upanishads that he believed to support his monotheistic construal of Hinduism. Although copies were rare in the United States during Rammohan's lifetime, tantalizing tidbits appeared in a Boston magazine as early as 1818, and heftier bites very soon came. These appetizers may have led some curious readers to translations of Sanskrit works by British orientalists, either excerpted in British magazines widely read in America, like the *Edinburgh Review,* or already available in local libraries. Boston possessed at least a few such texts. It should be remembered that the Massachusetts Historical Society had elected Sir William Jones a member and that Harvard College had begged him to send Indian manuscripts for its library.[6]

We know for sure that members of the most liberal wing of Unitarianism, the Transcendentalists, sought out Hindu texts — and went beyond them. Ralph Waldo Emerson read Sanskrit translations in the *Edinburgh Review* and the *Asiatic Journal* in the 1820s and 1830s and "worked his way through a list of books that offered detailed introductions to Oriental thought." In the 1840s his attention turned to Buddhism. He got pretty confused about it — not his fault, since westerners were then only starting to gain understanding of Buddhism and access to Buddhist texts. Around the same time, another Transcendentalist, Elizabeth Peabody, was giving lectures in Boston on the history of religions.[7] In the Transcendentalist journal, *The Dial*, during 1843 and 1844, Emerson, Peabody, and Henry Thoreau edited excerpts from Hindu, Confucian, Buddhist, Zoroastrian, and other ancient texts. They called this series "ethnical scriptures." (To a scholar today, it appears odd that the selections included the late-antique corpus attributed to the mythical Egyptian sage Hermes Trismegistus; that is, Thrice-Great Hermes. The *Gulistan — Rose Garden —* of the medieval Persian poet Sa'di also makes a slightly implausible candidate for 'scripture.') In the long run, the Transcendentalist desire to plunge westerners into "ethnical scriptures" culminated in a *Sacred Anthology* edited by Emerson's epigone Moncure Conway in 1874, a small-scale forerunner of Max Müller's *Sacred Books of the East*.[8]

But Transcendentalist writers explored such texts with very different aims than the previous Unitarian generation. The older Unitarians embraced Rammohan because he seemed close to their brand of Christianity. The Transcendentalists turned to their "ethnical scriptures" because they were searching for something beyond Christianity.

'Dissatisfaction with historic Christianity,' in fact, makes a pretty good, if partial, definition of Transcendentalism. The dissatisfaction very much included Unitarianism. To the Transcendentalists, their old faith — or large portions of it — came to seem a mythology descended from a more primitive age, with much of nobility but also much of cruelty in it, incapable of providing reliable knowledge of God.[9] The specific issue over which Emerson resigned from the ministry was the Lord's Supper, a ritual that he regarded as suited to "the people and the modes of thought" in the ancient oriental world, "full of idols and ordinances," but unfitted to a modern age.[10]

What might fit better? Transcendentalist study of non-European religions taught them that Christianity shared much with other religions. "Every reader knows," Emerson alleged (not very plausibly), "that almost every passage in our sacred books can be paralleled with a like sentiment from another book of a distant nation"; thus, "we find in our mythology[!] a key to theirs." All great religions amounted only to "well-meant approximations" to some grander divine truth; but, he said, we should not "censure" their failings but "point out the identity of their inspiration with every other inspiration." "There is but one Religion," wrote Emerson's friend Theodore Parker, "though many theologies."[11]

To approach more closely the truths of the "one Religion," the Transcendentalists believed, each individual had to learn to intuit spiritual realities within himself or herself — to hear the voice of God within, so to speak. Jesus, the Buddha, Zoroaster, and other great religious teachers surely had discovered the truths they uttered in exactly this way. This last axiom owed a lot more to the diluted German idealism that oozed through Transcendentalism than it did to any words actually uttered by Jesus, the Buddha, or Zoroaster. But the Transcendentalists' half-conscious realization of where their spiritual doctrine really came from did not make it any less compelling, at least to themselves. The most radical Unitarians, like Emerson and Parker, threw off the authority of the Bible, while affirming that spiritual jewels glowed among its dross. (Thoreau went further, actually preferring Asian religions over Christianity.[12]) They came to believe that 'pure' Christianity consisted in the voice of God in each individual heart. Creeds and institutions were transient, the love of God and of one's fellow human beings permanent. Truth appeared in every great religious tradition, half-buried under incrustations of human error. Most famously, Parker expounded this wish in his 1841 sermon "A Discourse of the Transient and Permanent in Christianity."[13]

Between wish and fulfillment fell awkward reality. Few human beings were heroes of spiritual insight like Jesus or the Buddha. So some guidance came in handy — and this is what Transcendentalists hoped to dig out of the study of non-European religions. They believed that every great religion contained glimpses of the divine truths that all religions sought. Hence it mattered to learn what non-Christian religions had to say and how their doctrines fit with Christian teaching. Such inquiries could illuminate the path to a higher, fuller religion — either the culmination of Christianity or the universal religion that would supersede Christianity and other world religions. And since error deformed every religion, it formed no obstacle to this quest that Hindus burned widows on their husbands' funeral pyres or that Zoroastrians seemed to worship fire — any more than that Jehovah ordered the Israelites to slaughter women and children or that more backward Unitarians still offered Communion. Thus Emerson looked to Hinduism and Buddhism (as he understood them) to flesh out his post-Christian universal religion within every person. The fact that Emerson's knowledge of Hinduism was touch-and-go, his knowledge of Buddhism close to zero, never interfered. The mysticism he perceived as central to Hinduism made that religion especially attractive.[14] Put differently, his intense interest in non-Christian religions grew almost entirely from his doubts about historic Christianity and his search for an alternative to it.

In levitating entirely above Christianity, Emerson went to the extreme. Not every Transcendentalist, and certainly not every Unitarian who leaned toward Transcendentalism, expected Christianity to fade away in the face of higher truth. Emerson's more learned parallel Theodore Parker, following a route close to Emerson's, never wanted Christianity to become obsolete. Parker read widely and thoughtfully about Asian religions. He concluded that Hinduism was not quite as bad as Calvinism but that a 'purified' Christianity beat all comers.[15] Yet he saw some truth in 'lesser' faiths, and he considered it needful to look into the relationship between Christianity and other widespread faiths of the world as a step in the process of purifying Christianity. Transcendentalists like him clung to an attenuated, residual Christianity, shorn of most of its historical particularity, while conceding a degree of truth in non-European religions and stressing the importance of learning about them. Though not exactly disinterested scholarship, this approach ultimately had big consequences for learning.

For between the 1820s and early 1870s, the handful of Americans who engaged respectfully, systematically, and at length with non-European religions — rather than dismissing them as idolatry — came from the circle of the Transcendentalists. True, a bevy of shorter writings perched on individual pieces of the puzzle. Among the learned, the Yale orientalist Edward E. Salisbury published several articles on aspects of Islam and on Buddhism; his even more accomplished student, William Dwight Whitney, wrote much Sanskrit scholarship, some of it bearing fairly directly on Hinduism. Salisbury himself fathered the *Journal of the American Oriental Society* shortly after the Society's founding in 1842.[16] It helped to bring knowledge of Islam, Hinduism, and Buddhism to well-educated readers, although this was not its main purpose. Its articles on Asian religions belonged to more general orientalist scholarship; studied for the most part either a special aspect of one religion or an ancient text (via translation or summary); and never aimed to present a comprehensive picture of non-European religions.[17] And the *Journal of the American Oriental Society* was caviar for the general. What most Americans read about Asia made no pretense of erudition. In sheer bulk, 'field reports' by Protestant missionaries lamenting indigenous religious practices in India or China dominated writing on Asian religions. In the *Chinese Repository*, for instance, published between 1832 and 1851, missionaries occasionally dealt with — usually to deprecate — Buddhism, but even the denunciations were ignorant.[18] No Americans other than writers from the vicinity of Transcendentalism ventured large-scale, serious, comparative investigations of non-European religions. I hesitate to say that all these authors *were* Transcendentalists, if only because so loose a movement provides too many moving targets. But all the writers in question at least hovered around Transcendentalists.

This background gave their way of studying non-European religions a family resemblance. There were four common traits. First, only religions with long histories and wide geographic spread interested them. A religion that had petered out after a few centuries or failed to attract adherents in many places seemed unlikely to contain a big dose of spiritual truth. Second, only religions of sophisticated, complex cultures, like those of China and India, got much attention. Transcendentalists were running away from what they regarded as primitive survivals in Christianity; they were hardly going to turn to Siberian shamans to find religious truth. (Put differently, they did not prefigure New Agers.) Third, for the most part, only religions grounded in authoritative texts that seemed parallel to the Bible counted as worth investigating. (At a time when Greek and Latin still lorded over the schooling of elite males, classical paganism got a pass on this precondition.) The quest to excavate universal truths in all faiths methodologically mandated, so to say, this insistence on 'sacred' texts. If you could not *read* each religion's truth-claims, how could you, sitting in Boston, learn what they were? The stress on "ethnical scriptures" also reflected a simple fact: long-lasting religions widespread in sophisticated cultures generally had such texts. Finally, the study of religions needed to take a comparative approach. Investigators could only discover truths common to all religions by lining them up next to each other.

A clear picture of this Unitarian-Transcendentalist approach to the comparative study of religion emerges from a tract composed in 1855–56. The author was a Boston-area Unitarian minister a little less radical than Parker, Thomas Wentworth Higginson (1823–1911). (He is better remembered as colonel of the First South Carolina Volunteers, a heroic regiment of ex-slaves in the Civil War, and as the pen pal who brought Emily Dickinson into print.) It may also signify for his interest in non-European religions that Higginson grew up knowing of India, his father being a merchant in the trade. According to his "Preliminary Note," Higginson drafted his essay as a chapter of a work tellingly "to be entitled 'The Return of Faith.'" Higginson never finished his book, and in 1871 he published this fragment under the equally telling title *The Sympathy of Religions*. Its aegis is also revealing. It appeared in *The Radical*, a magazine sponsored by the Free Religious Association, and also as an FRA pamphlet. The FRA was founded in 1867 by Transcendentalist-minded Unitarians who objected to the Christian affirmations of the newly created National Conference of Unitarian Churches. The organization housed an interesting tension between members who sought a 'scientific' basis for religious belief and those who brought a more traditional Transcendentalist idealism to the search for universal religion. Some FRA leaders, like Octavius Brooks

Frothingham (ironically the first historian of Transcendentalism) had gone beyond idealism to 'scientific theism.' Others, like Higginson, remained within the orbit of Transcendentalist thinking.[19]

Echoing Emerson and Parker, Higginson declared, "Our true religious life begins when we discover that there is an Inner Light, not infallible but invaluable, which 'lighteth every man that cometh into the world.'" But not every man professed Christianity; ergo, Christianity could hardly monopolize the light. Higginson continued,

> Every year brings new knowledge of the religions of the world, and every step in knowledge brings out the sympathy between them. They all show similar aims, symbols, forms, weaknesses, and aspirations. Looking at these points of unity, we might say that under many forms there is but one religion, whose essential creed is the Fatherhood of God, and the Brotherhood of Man [Unitarians often cited the Fatherhood of God and the Brotherhood of Man as the essential principles of their faith], — disguised by corruptions, symbolized by mythologies, ennobled by virtues, degraded by vices, but still the same.

The Bible, Higginson logically added, is incomplete in itself. "The time will come" when "all pious books will be called sacred scriptures." It is not clear how much Higginson really knew about, say, Buddhism (probably not much, given some of his assertions). But ignorance never saps optimism. "It is our happiness to live in a time when all religions are at last outgrowing their mythologies, and emancipated men are stretching out their hands to share together 'the luxury of a religion that does not degrade.'" "The great religions of the world," Higginson firmly believed, "share the same aspirations, and every step in the progress of each brings it nearer to all the rest."[20]

In effect, Higginson provided a prospectus for a comparative history of religion; the first American stab at the thing itself (if we do not count Hannah Adams's dictionary) was Lydia Maria Child's *Progress of Religious Ideas through Successive Ages*. Child published her three-volume book in 1855, just when Higginson was drafting his essay, probably unknown to her.[21] Child's (1802–80) own life made a compelling story. Born in 1802, she grew up under the intellectual tutelage of her older brother, Convers Francis, a Unitarian minister who moved in Transcendentalist circles. Maria Francis, as she was then called, became a friend in particular of Margaret Fuller, the Transcendentalist writer and early feminist. Maria later displayed her own feminism not only in her independent life but also in her *History of the Condition of Women in Various Ages and Nations* (1835). Maria taught in a girls' school while writing novels and children's literature on the side. In 1828, aged twenty-six, she married a Harvard-educated lawyer, David Child. Child introduced her to abolitionism, and Lydia Maria Child henceforth made antislavery her chief moral focus. Her husband proved a financial disaster, and Maria supported the household by writing, chiefly what we would now class as self-help books for women. (Maria and David separated for about a decade; during this period, she apparently supported only herself.) Her writing made her famous, until her abolitionist writings turned fame into infamy.

In the midst of all these difficulties, she turned out the *Progress of Religious Ideas*. This book, like Hannah Adams's dictionary, was a much needed potboiler.[22] But the *Progress of Religious Ideas* also showed Child's genuine concern for religious toleration — an archetypal Unitarian position — as well as her considerable though hardly comprehensive reading. The book, she said, took "more than eight years" to write. But she was writing other things simultaneously, and her source base was not impressive and tilted heavily toward books about Christianity. To take a representative example,

Child's 138 pages on Hinduism rely on a mere nine titles — none disreputable, but altogether highly eclectic. Her catch-as-catch-can research may well reflect her residence during these years in Wayland, now a Boston suburb but then fairly remote from Boston and Cambridge libraries.[23]

Nonetheless, Child's coverage was far more balanced than the sources available to her. She epitomized her point of view in the epigraph she chose for the title page, lines from the poet James Russell Lowell, yet another writer from a Unitarian background influenced by Transcendentalism:

> God sends his teachers unto every age,
> To every clime, and every race of men,
> With revelations fitted to their growth
> And shape of mind, nor gives the realm of TRUTH
> Into the selfish rule of one sole race:
> Therefore, each form of worship that hath swayed
> The life of man, and given it to grasp
> The master-key of knowledge, REVERENCE,
> Enfolds some germs of goodness and of right.

Like Hannah Adams, Child insisted that she strove to present the truth-claims of all religions without prejudice or denigration. Unlike Adams, she specifically abjured the Christian habit of explaining away "apparent contradictions and absurdities, in Jewish or Christian writings, with a veil of allegories and mystical interpretation" while snickering at similar irrationality in other religions. In short, in comparing religions, Child tried to place all of them "precisely on a level" with Christianity. In contrast, Hannah Adams had aimed mainly to provide an encyclopedia of Christian disagreements and only tacked on her listing of non-Christian religions. Child did not write from a post-Christian angle, but in studying other faiths she did mean (like Higginson) to abstract herself from her own liberal Christian beliefs and to treat "all religions with reverence." This intention made *The Progress of Religious Ideas* a pathbreaking kind of work in the United States.[24]

Child's work showed its quasi-Transcendentalist background in another respect. Like Emerson, Peabody, and Thoreau before her, and like Higginson writing simultaneously, Child took as the proper basis for understanding non-European religions their "own Sacred Books." Child's principle may have owed something to her brother, Convers Francis, an enthusiast for compiling a 'world Bible,' though the idea was widespread in the Transcendentalist circles in which she had circulated. She tried to read the 'scriptures' of non-European religions with something like what we would call a historicist approach; that is, she saw them as products of long-ago cultures, of particular times and places. The "modern mind, so foreign to ancient habits of thought, and separated from them by the lapse of ages," could grasp the meaning of such sacred texts only with great care and necessarily imperfectly. This historicist notion was recent, but current, in New England Unitarian scholarly circles. Indeed Child may have picked up her historicism indirectly from her brother's teacher at the Unitarian Harvard Divinity School, the biblical critic Andrews Norton. In contrast, more orthodox American Protestants, even so learned a man as Presbyterian Princeton's Charles Hodge, as conversant as Norton with recent German biblical scholarship, still tended to treat the Bible as essentially transparent to modern readers.[25]

The focus on "Sacred Books," or "ethnical scriptures," and on the difficulty of interpreting them gave a distinctive character to the comparative study of religions. Transcendentalists and near-Transcendentalists like Child wrote more or less discontented with traditional, orthodox Christianity. Their interest in non-European religions came from a wish to explore alternatives to Christianity in the hope either of going beyond it (Emerson) or of reforming it drastically (Parker). The final chapter of Child's work devoted itself to this project. She traced the "progress of religious ideas" (note: *ideas*, not practices or experiences) through all ages (and through her own interminable verbiage) in order to show the essential sameness of basic religious truths under their various forms. She thus demonstrated, or believed she had, the potential convergence of all major religions into a form more adequate to the time.[26]

Now, if you are examining other faiths in order to find intricate religious ideas that might emend and expand Christian theology, then you have to read the "Sacred Books" associated with these non-European religions. Religions lacking such texts may embody complex world views. One thinks, for instance, of Siberian shamanism or of American Indian religions, practiced by peoples without writing (at least for most of their histories). But it is hard to excavate the clear, detailed structure of a complex symbolic system without written texts to dig into. Yet Transcendentalists and their ilk sought precisely ideas comparable to Christian theology. Greek and Roman paganism lacked texts functioning exactly like the Bible or Qur'an, although many of the ancients approached the Homeric epics as sacred texts.[27] But even apart from Homer, classical paganism produced a wealth of explanatory commentaries on the gods ranging from Hesiod to Cicero.

And so Child wrote at length about ancient paganism — and about ancient Egyptian religion, Hinduism, Buddhism, Confucianism, Zoroastrianism, Judaism, Christianity, and Islam. She barely glanced at the textless religions of ancient Celtic and Mesopotamian peoples. (Scholars had deciphered Egyptian hieroglyphs roughly a quarter century before Child wrote, whereas the texts bearing on ancient Mesopotamian religion, notably the epic of Gilgamesh, awaited discovery.) She completely ignored the tribal religions existing in her own time. To put this point more concisely, Child focused on what students of comparative religion would soon call the World Religions.

The next American to write a comprehensive narrative of comparative religion followed Child's example. This author was, it almost goes without saying, another Unitarian of Transcendentalist leanings: the Reverend James Freeman Clarke (1810–88). Clarke's book was far more erudite than Child's (he did not need to write quickly to keep his pantry full), far more academic, and far more influential. Conrad Cherry records that it went through eighteen reprintings. Indeed Clarke's *Ten Great Religions: An Essay in Comparative Theology*, first published in 1871, appears among the founding texts of the academic study of religions in standard histories of the field. Even Max Müller nodded to Clarke in the Urtext, his 1873 *Introduction to the Science of Religion*. A more specialized study in comparative religion had actually intervened between Child's and Clarke's works: *A Critical History of the Doctrine of a Future Life* (1860) by yet another Unitarian minister (and Horatio Alger's cousin), the minor Transcendentalist William Rounseville Alger (1822–1905). The second part of his five-section work, devoted to "Ethnic Thoughts concerning a Future Life," surveyed everything from druidical and Etruscan to Zoroastrian and Islamic thoughts on the subject. Clarke acknowledged "Alger's admirable monograph" as the only American work of comparative theology "worthy of notice."[28] But Alger did not aspire to comprehensive comparison of religions, as Child and Clarke did.

Clarke looks to us (as he did to Max Müller) more like a serious student of religions than Child does; yet he wrote from a virtually identical point of view. A product of Harvard College and Harvard Divinity School, Clarke — we can already guess — hobnobbed with Transcendentalists. He even dared to exchange pulpits with Theodore Parker, who had been ostracized by more conventional Unitarian ministers. During a stint as pastor of a Unitarian church in

Louisville, Clarke published from 1833 to 1836 the *Western Messenger*, a journal that historians regard as the first Transcendentalist periodical. Like other liberal Unitarians, he believed in the permanent upward progress of humankind toward a fuller and deeper grasp of spiritual and moral truths. It comes, then, as no surprise at all that he developed a strong interest in non-European religions. In them, one might observe the patterns of this progress and the obstacles to it. "We can never understand the nature of a phenomenon," he wrote, "when we contemplate it by itself, as well as when we look at it in its relations to other phenomena of the same kind. The qualities of each become more clear in contrast with those of the others."[29] This is why Clarke gave *Ten Great Religions* the subtitle *An Essay in Comparative Theology* — and why he focused on the textual traditions of these religions and on the propositional truth-claims and explicit moral prescriptions found in these texts.

Clarke knew that other kinds of religions existed. In 1883 he published a sequel to *Ten Great Religions*, based on Lowell Lectures he gave in 1881–82. He organized this book around widespread religious themes such as the idea of God, the soul, prayer and worship, and the origin of the world. In it, Clarke did deal with textless religions — in his terms "the religions of the primitive or childlike races" — fitting them into his overall schema of human progress "from monotony [he thought all "Tribal" religions essentially alike], through variety, to an ultimate harmony." But 'primitive' religion remained only propaedeutic to the understanding of the 'great' religions that really mattered.[30]

The original *Ten Great Religions* started life in 1868 as six articles in elite Boston's journal of record, the *Atlantic Monthly*; but Clarke said that he "had made of this study a speciality" for over twenty-five years. For the book version published in the spring of 1871, he expanded the original articles and added four new chapters.[31] Tellingly, the original articles dealt with Confucianism, Hinduism, Buddhism,

Zoroastrianism, and ancient Egyptian religion. Clarke did not get around to the more familiar territory of Judaism, Christianity, and Islam, plus Greek and Roman paganism, until the chapters added in the book version. (He also dealt then with Scandinavian mythology, becoming well known to learned Americans in Clarke's lifetime.) He thus reversed the previous pattern of giving priority to the well-known Religions of the Book and of the classical schoolroom in favor of highlighting Asian religions.

Clarke's novelty also lay in offering a *scholarly* comparative study of religion, the first such synthesis written in the United States. He barely beat out Samuel Johnson's three-volume *Oriental Religions*; Johnson, another liberal Unitarian minister influenced by Transcendentalism, outmatched Clarke in erudition but fell far short in readership.[32] *Ten Great Religions* did not involve original research. Clarke lacked the languages to undertake his own investigations of Buddhism or Confucianism; but he did read French and German, and his book (like Johnson's) amounted largely to a reprocessing of European scholarship. Clarke let his readers know this, promising "to give the latest results of modern investigations" and trolling names of celebrated European philologists like Friedrich Max Müller, Eugène Burnouf, Ernest Renan, and Georg Friedrich Creuzer. Clarke's grasp of the "latest" scholarship sometimes faltered, but he made the best stab any American had to date. Clarke warmly applauded Lydia Maria Child's book, generously attributing its inadequacies to "the few sources of information then accessible." This excuse held some truth, but it would have been more accurate, if less kind, to point out that an elite Boston minister had more access to the latest erudition, and more leisure to absorb it, than did a woman scrabbling to make a living from her pen in rural Wayland. In any case, Clarke knew the lay of the scholarly land well enough to do something Child had never dreamed of: to position his "science" of comparative theology among the comparative sciences then at the height of their prestige — comparative anatomy, comparative geography, and above all, comparative philology. Like these other fields of study, comparative theology "may be called a science, since it consists in the study of the facts of human history, and their relation to each other. It does not dogmatize: it observes. It deals only with phenomena, — single phenomena, or facts; grouped phenomena, or laws."[33]

Yet for all his erudite veneer Clarke pursued the same goal as his Transcendentalist predecessors. Comparative theology aimed to "examine the different religions to find wherein each is complete or defective, true or false; how each may supply the defects of the other or prepare the way for a better; how each religion acts on the race which receives it, is adapted to that race, and to the region of the earth which it inhabits." Comparative theology "shows the relation of each *partial* religion to human civilization, and observes how each religion of the world is a step in the progress of humanity. It shows that both the positive and negative side of a religion make it a preparation for a higher religion, and that the universal religion must root itself in the decaying soil of partial religions."[34] One can almost hear Emerson singing in the chorus.

But if Emerson had read a few pages further along, he would have shut his mouth; for Clarke was traditional enough to believe that this universal religion to come would be a cleansed Christianity — not, certainly, the warped, corrupted Christianity of Emerson's and Clarke's Calvinist ancestors, but a purified, spiritualized Christianity. Clarke could find something good to say about almost all of the other world religions. (Very traditionally, he excoriated Islam.) Non-European religions "must contain more truth than error, and must have been, on the whole, useful to mankind." Otherwise, none of them could have held "its position in the world during so long a time and over so wide a range." But all the other "great religions" each expressed at best only one important aspect of faith. Buddhism, for example, was "the Protestantism of the East." "Christianity is adapted to take their place, not because they are false, but because they are true as far as they go."[35]

Clarke drew a sharp distinction between "ethnic" religions, each adapted to the "special religious qualities" of one "race" of human-kind, and a "catholic" religion, "adapted to become the Religion of all Races." (In the 1883 sequel he added "Tribal" religions to his sequence.) "Christianity, from the first, showed itself capable of taking possession of the convictions of the most different races" — a fact symbolized in the "miracle of tongues" on Pentecost. "Christianity alone, of all human religions, seems to possess the power of keeping abreast with the advancing civilization of the world." As it progressed, then, Christianity would in fact "become the Religion of all Races." Like Higginson, Clarke believed the human race headed toward an evolving universal creed that would one day absorb and transcend all faiths, including Christianity in its present form. Unlike Higginson, he believed Christianity alone could and would provide the foundation of this future faith.[36]

Let us stand back and examine in longer perspective the first real foundations of the academic study of religion in the United States — that is to say, these Unitarian writings, inflected by Transcendentalism. Two points need emphasis. One involves motive, and that is the tension between commitment to Christianity and longing for a universal religion to displace or to perfect a Christianity that some of these inquirers found no longer entirely plausible. The whole purpose in comparing Christianity with non-European religions was to find materials with which either to replace it or to repair it. The second point involves method, and that is the stress on applying the comparative method to the so-called World Religions, religions distinguished by the central role in them of canonical texts.

If we look across the Atlantic in the 1870s, we find exactly the same method applied by the Anglo-German pioneer of religious studies, Oxford's Friedrich Max Müller. Müller in fact devoted the largest share of his time in the last twenty-five years of his life to editing a series called *The Sacred Books of the East*. These translations of canonical texts of Hinduism, Buddhism, Taoism, Confucianism, Zoroastrianism, and Islam, ultimately ran to fifty volumes — a series that Müller referred to as "my *Bibliotheca Sacra*" or "sacred library." Thus was fulfilled Higginson's prophecy that in due time "all pious books will be called sacred scriptures." Müller intended to include the Old and New Testaments until more prudent colleagues warned him that lumping Christian scriptures with the Qur'an and the Avesta might ruffle certain sensibilities.[37]

Thus, American writers comparing religions converged in method with the European leader — indeed definer — of the new field. From early in the twentieth century, historians of religious studies have numbered among their ancestors such investigators of tribal religions as Edward Burnett Tylor. And religion did occupy most of the pages of Tylor's *Primitive Culture* (1871). But Tylor is also remembered as a founder of anthropology, and in his own day that discipline is where 'primitive' religion belonged. In 1893 the section of the École Pratique des Hautes Études dealing with *sciences religieuses* added teaching on the religions of "peuples non civilisés." This expanded the new discipline's field of view — though scholars in the anglophone world did not hurry to follow suit. The *Introduction to the History of Religions* (1913) by Harvard's Crawford H. Toy was exceptional in devoting itself mostly to 'primitive' religions — though even here in order to show the "principal customs and ideas that underlie all public religion," with the "lines of progress" leading to "the higher religions." Likewise, William Robertson Smith's fascination with primitive totemism in *The Religion of the Semites* (1889) mattered because learning about these earlier cults was supposed to illuminate the Old Testament. And like Smith, his disciple James G. Frazer used comparative data from 'primitive' religions to elucidate the origins of a 'civilized' religion (in his case Greek and Roman paganism). On both sides of the Atlantic, the emerging discipline of comparative religion took as its major focus the study of 'sacred,' or at least canonical, texts.[38]

Yet appearances can deceive. Max Müller had arrived at the comparative study of religious texts from Sanskrit studies and comparative philology (also called comparative historical grammar). When Müller developed his philology into comparative religion, he inflected it (or infected it) with his idiosyncratic, if not wacky, mysticism. But the roots of his version of religious studies ran deep into philological scholarship, and his original motive for undertaking work on the Vedas had nothing to do with his own diminishing religious beliefs.[39] Likewise, William Robertson Smith started from philological study of the Hebrew scriptures, and James G. Frazer's *Golden Bough* began from classical philology. Put succinctly, comparative religion in the United Kingdom grew from a solidly established tradition of philological scholarship, which circumscribed and restrained even personal religious concerns. Nothing like this ballast existed in the United States. The origins of American study of comparative religion reflected instead the anxieties and hopes of a liberalizing Protestantism.

And although Unitarians, the most liberal Protestants, pioneered the new studies in the United States, after 1871 an interest in the systematic study of non-European religions spread rapidly to other Protestants, usually protomodernists. A good deal of this new writing comparing religions pivoted on the missionary enterprise. As early as 1845, a canny Yale professor warned his fellow Congregationalists that missionaries needed to adapt "Christian truth to the heathen mind" to assure the "thorough triumph" of the true faith; and such "adaptation" required study of the "religious systems of heathenism."[40] Liberal Protestants tended to reject traditional notions that 'heathenism' sprang from "the lower and depraved tastes of humanity" or even from the work of the devil, best eradicated root and branch.[41] The Reverend John Henry Barrows (1847–1902), a liberal Presbyterian minister in Chicago, chaired the committee that organized the celebrated World's Parliament of Religions at the Chicago World's Fair in 1893, an event that included some forty spokespersons for Asian religions. The experience transformed Barrows into an advocate of interreligious understanding. He, much like Clarke, maintained the superiority of Christianity. But as Barrows's biographer wrote, he also warned against "denigration of other religions and cultures." Although Barrows felt sure that Protestantism would triumph "as the final form of all religion," sensitivity to other world faiths "would allow Protestantism to express itself in new ways and to expand in new places."[42]

By the late nineteenth century, then, religious motivations for comparing religions covered a spectrum. They ranged from the moderate conviction that missionary success depended on knowledge of and respect for non-Christian religions to the post-Christian belief that all great faiths were essentially equivalent. These shifting Protestant attitudes initially thrust the project of comparing religions into new prominence in the United States — in sharp contrast to the origin of the scientific study of religion in Europe.

Slipshod tracts like Higginson's opened the door for serious scholarship on the subject. Around such heightened curiosity developed a new American academic discipline. It aimed to classify faiths systematically into distinct types and to investigate their relationships, based on erudite study of individual faith traditions by trained scholars. But its course followed that set by nonacademic writers such as James Freeman Clarke: comparative study of the sacred texts of the great World Religions — what Clarke called "comparative theology." The new field also absorbed the Unitarian notion that religions evolved from the more primitive to the more advanced — an idea easy to accept in the late nineteenth-century heyday of evolutionism. So the new academic discipline pretty closely replicated the older nonacademic, Unitarian study of religions from which it itself evolved. This intellectualist view of religion provoked William James to offer a new paradigm for religious studies, as we shall see in the last chapter.

William James Redraws the Map

In the last quarter of the nineteenth century, a new humanistic discipline devoted to the study of religion took shape in the United States. To be sure, the academic discipline did not stem a continuing current of popular interest, on which drifted a motley flotilla of old-fashioned, unscholarly texts.[1] And while the university set a more professional standard, it could not agree on a name for the new studies. Many of the first scholars in this new discipline called their field 'history of religions.' 'Science of religion' also enjoyed some currency. In the course of the twentieth century, 'science of religion' largely fell out of use in North America, replaced by 'religious studies' or even simply 'religion.' Another term in common use for the discipline was and is 'comparative religion.' I prefer this last label because it highlights the comparative method central to the field in its beginnings. The comparative method descended from philology, but the family tree is far too gnarled to trace in these pages.[2]

For our purposes, the origin of the comparative method matters less than the reason for adopting it. As we have seen, in the United States — unlike Europe — the discipline of religious studies was born from a felt need to measure Christianity against alternatives. Such comparison aimed either to make Christianity more persuasive to the 'heathens' or to perfect Christianity by locating the elements of a universal religion common to all peoples. American writers about non-European religions, from Hannah Adams onward, depended on European books for their information. As comparative religion began to infiltrate universities in the United States in the late nine-teenth and early twentieth centuries, American scholars looked to Europe for appropriately academic methodological models as well.[3] Yet most of these same Americans were still driven by their indig-enous motive for bothering to study religion in the first place.

When *exactly* they got a proper discipline for studying it was never clear.[4] No great event stands out to mark the birth of the academic study of religion. But the floodgates opened in the early 1870s — granted, floodgates in a tiny dam. James Freeman Clarke's *Ten Great Religions* of 1871 was immediately followed by a *Comparative History of Religions* by Princeton Seminary's James C. Moffat — the very Moffat who twenty years earlier had written so winsomely of "the midnight blackness of Hindooism." His new book suffered from a badly split personality, a type of psychosis not unusual in the new discipline. Moffat designed the work as apologetics to show that "the essential principles inherent" in all religions lead not only to Christianity but, quite specifically, to Calvinist Christianity. At the same time, he knew a good deal of the European learned literature, such as Burnouf on Buddhism; and his handling of material was scholarly in tone, not overtly propa-gandistic or proselytizing.[5] In the following year, as mentioned be-fore, appeared the first volume of Samuel Johnson's trilogy *Oriental Religions*, treating India. Then in 1873 the new Boston University created a "professor of comparative history of religion, comparative theology, and philosophy of religion," apparently the first American professorship in the field.[6]

But the longest American tradition of instruction in non-European religions belonged to Harvard's Divinity School. As early as 1854 students heard lectures on comparative religion from James Freeman Clarke; and he returned in 1867 for a four-year stint. Charles Carroll Everett (1829–1900) succeeded him in 1872, lectur-ing on comparative religion from a more specifically Hegelian point of view but with equally Christian intent. Everett ended his career as dean of the Divinity School, and he was followed by Crawford Toy (1836–1919), primarily a Semitic philologist. The Divinity School officially got a professorship in the new field in 1904 when George F. Moore was named Frothingham Professor of the History of Religions.[7]

This instruction at Harvard explicitly formed part of training for the Christian ministry, and so did the rest of the earliest teaching of comparative religion in the United States. James C. Moffat taught church history in Princeton Theological Seminary. The professor of comparative history of religion, et cetera, et cetera, in Boston University was a Methodist minister, William Fairfield Warren (also the university's president). Warren had studied in Germany, and he published serious books on ancient cosmologies. But he wrote from Christian presuppositions; he tilted toward Christian apologetics rather than disinterested scholarship; and he taught in the university's School of Theology. New York University lacked a theological seminary; but that did not prevent it from appointing the Reverend Frank Ellinwood, a Presbyterian missionary leader, as its first professor of comparative religion in 1887. In 1890 Ellinwood even founded the American Society of Comparative Religion (which never actually stretched past the Hudson). Protestant ministers filled all its offices. Ellinwood's students came from nearby divinity schools. Four got doctorates under his supervision — three local pastors and the secretary of the New York Bible Society. When Ellinwood lectured on Asian religions in 1891 at Union Theological Seminary, he titled his opening talk "The Need of Understanding the False Religions."

Cornell seems to have been the first American institution to teach the history of religions outside of the context of ministerial training, starting in 1891. It was not the proudest moment in Cornell's distinguished history. The professor, Charles Mellen Tyler, was the pastor of a Congregationalist church in Ithaca, foisted on the university by a major donor. Tyler published little, and that little reflected his insistent Christian commitments and his utter innocence of scholarly background or intentions.[8]

If we draw the veil of compassion over Cornell's shame, university work in comparative religion independent of ministerial training began a year later. The University of Chicago, soon after opening its doors in 1892, set up a department of comparative religion in the Division of the Humanities. George S. Goodspeed (1860–1905), an expert on ancient Mesopotamia probably best remembered for his *History of the Babylonians and Assyrians* (1902), headed the new unit. Goodspeed also apparently provided its sole permanent faculty member at first. The department added in 1894 a lecturer on comparative religion, John Henry Barrows, of whom more will soon be said. In the same year it gave its first PhD, to Edmund Buckley, who defended a thesis on "Phallicism in Japan" and was promptly hired as a docent specialized in Asian religion. In 1899 the department awarded its second doctorate, to Laetitia Moon Conard with a dissertation on "Ideas of the Future Life Held by Algonkin Indian Tribes" — a piece of research respectable enough to be translated and published in two parts in the leading French journal of the new discipline, *Revue de l'histoire des religions*.[9]

By then, however, scholars in Europe probably regarded the University of Pennsylvania as offering the most professional approach to religious studies in the United States. Penn had pioneered in Mesopotamian archaeology, and this led to the establishment of a European-style, nontheological department of Semitic languages in 1897. Comparative religion began to be taught at Penn in the context of the Semitics program — even before the department was formally created — by Morris Jastrow. Jastrow, Polish by birth and American by upbringing, had studied in Leiden with Cornelius P. Tiele, a towering figure in the new discipline of religious studies. An accomplished scholar in his own right, Jastrow first taught courses in the history of religions (his mentor's preferred label for the field) in 1894. Neither erudition nor brilliance guarantees an audience, and a paucity of students kept him from offering a formal course on the subject again until 1908. Still, in 1910 the university officially authorized graduate study in the history of religions.[10]

In these early decades few academic positions were exclusively devoted to the new discipline. Comparative religion did not implant itself widely until after the Second World War. Before then the few new PhDs often had trouble getting permanent jobs. But by 1900 or so the field had taken its place as a recognized academic discipline. Already in the 1890s the *New York Times* noted "the growing interest in this country and abroad in the historical study of religions," calling it "one of the noticeable features in the intellectual phases of past decades." An experienced textbook publisher (Ginn and Co.) judged then that the tide of curiosity had risen high enough to float a series, Handbooks on the History of Religions — manuals meant to "serve as textbooks for the historical study of religions in universities and seminaries."[11]

Textbooks presuppose professors, and they arrived by various routes. The Sanskrit scholar E. Washburn Hopkins (1857–1932), after postgraduate study in Germany, started his publishing career with closely focused monographs on the caste system in India, not to mention a study of the dog in the Rig Veda. But he soon widened his focus and produced the first academic general study in English of the history of Indian religions (1895). In that same year he succeeded the great William Dwight Whitney at Yale. Hopkins went on to still broader topics in *History of Religions* (1918) and *Origin and Evolution of Religion* (1923).[12] But his career path proved the exception.

Most scholars of comparative religion emerged from theology or biblical studies. Samuel Henry Kellogg (1839–1899), a Princeton Seminary graduate, started out teaching Presbyterian theology in

India. He became fluent in Hindi and conversant with Indian religions, then returned to America to publish *The Genesis and Growth of Religion* (1892) and a once-standard *Handbook of Comparative Religion* (1899). His *The Light of Asia and the Light of the World* (1885) compared Buddha and Christ. (*The Light of Asia* was the title of Sir Edwin Arnold's popular versified biography of Buddha, issued in 1879.) Kellogg published Old Testament criticism as well as comparative religion. Crawford Toy brought out a well-regarded history of religion in 1913; but the bulk of his work concerned the Bible, and his Harvard appointments were as Hancock Professor of Hebrew and Dexter Lecturer on Biblical Literature. George Foot Moore (1851–1931) was a major conduit for German biblical criticism; he went from professor of Old Testament at Andover Seminary (1883–1902) to professor of history of religion at Harvard (1902–28). There with his biblical hand he wrote *Judaism in the First Centuries of the Christian Era* (1927–30) and with his comparativist hand a major *History of Religions* (1913–19) — all the while remaining skeptical about a 'science' of comparative religion. Morris Jastrow of the University of Pennsylvania stood out from the crowd in being Jewish, in having studied with C. P. Tiele, and in importing into America Tiele's phenomenological approach to the historical study of religions. Jastrow was distinctly the most 'European' of the American pioneers of the discipline. (The Englishman Havelock Ellis recruited him to write the religious-studies volume for Ellis's Contemporary Science Series, dominated by European authors.) Yet Jastrow, too, had been ordained; and he regarded himself as "a specialist in Arabic, Assyrian, and rabbinical literature in connection with biblical exegesis."[13]

Since the University of Chicago offered the first respectable program in religious studies separated from ministerial training (as well as the first American PhD in it), it may prove instructive to take a closer look at what went on in Hyde Park. As already

mentioned, the Department of Comparative Religion began almost with the university itself in 1892. In fact, the person who
went on to write the first history of the new discipline, a Canadian
Presbyterian minister named Louis Henry Jordan (1855–1923),
started his prolific scholarly career at Chicago as special lecturer in
comparative religion around 1893.[14] The founder of Chicago's department, George S. Goodspeed, served as a Baptist pastor before
entering academe. Thereafter he doubled as biblical scholar and
Assyriologist.

In 1894 a donor expanded the study of religion at Chicago by
endowing the new lectureship in comparative religion. Its founding purpose was to expound on "the Relations of Christianity to
the Other Faiths of the World." Later that year the same donor
endowed a second lectureship, to be delivered every third year *in
India*, so that "in a friendly, temperate, conciliatory way . . . the
great questions of the truths of Christianity, its harmonies with
the truths of other religions, its rightful claims, and the best methods of setting them forth, should be presented to the scholarly and
thoughtful people of India." Both of these lectureships "came out
of the interest awakened by" the celebrated World Parliament of
Religions at the 1893 Chicago World's Fair. The first lecturer in both
of these new posts was the liberal Presbyterian minister who had
chaired the Parliament of Religions, John Henry Barrows. Indeed,
the adoring donor named the lectures to be delivered in India the
Barrows Lectures. (The proliferation of Presbyterian ministers at
the University of Chicago seems a little odd, the university being
a Baptist foundation.) Barrows went on to become president of
Oberlin College and to publish *Christianity, the World Religion*
(1897) and *The Christian Conquest of Asia* (1899). The titles make
crystal clear his point of view on non-European religions.[15] It does
not take prolonged investigation to discover that, in the United
States, comparative religion originated from Christian concerns.

What matters more, in its early years the discipline remained closely tied to the academic world of Christian theology and biblical studies. It was entirely characteristic that on the title page of his *Handbook of Comparative Religion* (1915), Samuel H. Kellogg titled himself simply "Missionary to India." Levi Leonard Paine, wearing his hat as professor of ecclesiastical history at Bangor Theological Seminary in Maine, wrote a book on the historical development of Christian trinitarianism. But he followed it up with another called *The Ethnic Trinities and Their Relations to the Christian Trinity: A Chapter in the Comparative History of Religions* (1901). The book opened by locating its version of the "comparative history of religions" squarely within the domain of "historical science" — presumably as distinct from apologetics or theology. Paine then went on to argue — relying "entirely on the scientific inductive method" — that earlier 'trinities' found in Hinduism, Zoroastrianism, and ancient Greek thought formed stages in a "world-wide historical evolution" culminating in Christian trinitarianism. Trinitarianism thus became one of the "divine revelations that are given in nature and history." As we have seen, the Christian connection remained strong even in institutional contexts formally divorced from theological seminaries, such as Chicago's. Even at Penn, after Morris Jastrow died in 1921, faculty from neighboring divinity schools soon took over the teaching of the history of religions.[16] It is helpful to remember the origin of the American Academy of Religion, the learned society for religious studies, founded as recently as 1964. It grew *not* from Ellinwood's ill-fated American Society of Comparative Religion (which vanished without a trace around 1900), but from the National Association of Biblical Instructors.

Not surprisingly, then, the new discipline aped its nonacademic Unitarian pioneers in one key respect. It assumed a paradigm of development from 'lower' to 'higher' religions; and it focused sharply on the latter, on religions with canonical texts and geographic reach more or less comparable to Christianity's. That is, comparative religion took for its animating concern the recently named World Religions.[17] Indeed, the two volumes of Moffat's early book were subtitled *Ancient Scriptures* and *Later Scriptures: Progress, and Revolutions of Faith*.

This is not to say that American scholars totally neglected other religions. By 1900 the religions of tribal peoples had become part of the standard fodder of the field in Europe and could hardly be avoided — and yet they did not quite fit. Look, for example, at Louis Henry Jordan's *Comparative Religion: Its Genesis and Growth* (1905), the first full-scale history of the discipline. Jordan included the study of what he called primitive religions, but he was not quite sure what to do with them. He wavered between taking such research as a proper part of comparative religion and treating investigations of these so-called anthropological religions as an auxiliary science. For the most part, American scholars subsumed tribal religions *under* the study of World Religions as a kind of preparatory sub-discipline. If the 'primitive' religions in question were those of the ancient Middle East, then they became part of the context within which developed Israelite religion and ultimately Christianity. The celebrated Scottish philologist William Robertson Smith had taken this approach; and in America Morris Jastrow, for example, followed it. Harvard's Crawford Toy exemplified the standard treatment of other tribal religions, what he called "the lower and the outlying cults, Australian, Negro [that is, African], North American Indian, Mexican, Peruvian," and so forth. These religions needed study because in them were found "*ideas* which are important for the understanding of higher systems" — that is, the "germinal forms of religion."[18] In short, 'primitive' religions mattered only when they somehow cast light on the 'scripture'-based World Religions at the center of the stage.

This stress on explicit 'theology' and ethics enabled George Foot Moore to articulate in 1913 an idea very close to the conception that Karl Jaspers in 1949 labeled the Axial Age, and to do so before Max Weber published the works supposed to have influenced Jaspers's thinking. It is worth quoting Moore at length, if only to scotch Eric Sharpe's assertion that Americans "of the scholarly status of W. D. Whitney, James Freeman Clarke and George Foot Moore" could make no "*distinctively American* contribution to the comparative study of religion" in its early years:

> Thereupon a new kind of religion arises in which men ask, not to be satisfied with the good things of this life, but to be exalted above the limitations of humanity or to be saved from the consequences of deeds, and, positively, to share the blessedness of the gods or to attain to union with the godhead. Salvation may be sought — to adopt the Indian analysis — by the way of works, or of knowledge, or of faith; and the methods vary accordingly. Religions of this type address themselves to the individual, and are therefore, logically, ways of salvation for all men, without distinction of nation or race; they often form organised religious communities and spread by missionary effort; the teachings of the founders are collected in a canon of authoritative scriptures and systematised in a body of doctrine, practical or philosophical.
>
> The great religions of this class have their beginnings in the centuries from the eighth to the fifth before the Christian era. This is the age of Taoism in China; of the Upanishads, of Buddhism, and of the precursors of Hinduism in India; of Zoroaster in Iran; of the Orphic-Pythagorean movement in Greece; and of the Hebrew prophets.[19]

One wonders if Jaspers had read Moore's widely circulated book.

Comparative religion during its first academic decades in the United States was thus a historically minded, text-based study oriented toward articulated religious or ethical propositions.[20] And the discipline's driving motive, stated or unstated, was to understand how non-European religions stacked up against Christianity. Samuel Kellogg thus organized the main chapters of his *Handbook of Comparative Religion* around individual "doctrines" in various religions paralleling the main tenets of Christianity; for instance, "The Doctrine of the World-Religions Concerning God" and "The Doctrine Concerning Salvation."[21] Even a comparative overview less insistently Christian than Kellogg's, Moore's *History of Religions*, stressed "religious *conceptions*, as they are implicit in myth and ritual or are thought out by poets, philosophers, and prophets; and particularly . . . the higher developments in theology, ethics, and religious philosophy." James Freeman Clarke's preferred label for the new discipline, comparative theology, hit pretty close to the mark.[22]

Into this new field of study, in June 1902, dropped an alien visitor from outer space. In that month appeared William James's *The Varieties of Religious Experience*. The book contained twenty chapters originally delivered as the Gifford Lectures on Natural Religion at the University of Edinburgh in 1901–02. The lectures comprised two sets of ten lectures each. James said he originally intended to devote the first ten to a description of "Man's Religious Appetites" and the second to the "Satisfaction" of these appetites "through Philosophy." And, indeed, the interplay of philosophy and religion had deeply engaged James in the years immediately preceding the invitation to deliver the Gifford Lectures. "But," he went on, "the unexpected growth of the psychological material," as he actually wrote the lectures, crowded out the intended ten philosophical lectures. The resulting volume thus formed a psychological study of what James called "the religious temperament," a book "loaded . . . with concrete examples" of this disposition's "extremer expressions."[23]

The Varieties of Religious Experience attracted a lot of attention the moment it appeared, and it has continued to do so in the

century since James died. I do not pretend to control the vast literature on James; but so far as I can see, commentators have focused
on three issues in the book. The first is the methodological question of whether investigating what James himself called "extremer
expressions" of religious faith really provides evidence of religion as
a *general* phenomenon. Early reviewers fretted a lot over this problem. But once *Varieties* — as I shall henceforth call it — entered the
canon of classic works, this controversy died down. When we recognize a book as a monument, we stop worrying about its solidity. The
second issue is James's ontological division of religion into two basic
types: what he labeled the healthy-minded and the sick souls, also
known as the once-born and the twice-born. James borrowed this
distinction from Francis Newman, John Henry Newman's younger
brother, who coined the latter pair of opposites in the 1840s as
he himself was moving away from evangelical Protestantism into
a vague, nondoctrinal theism.[24] This distinction still evokes discussion, as does the third issue: the epistemological question of
whether James's pragmatist interpretation of religious experience
can or cannot ground the truth of the unseen in any meaningful
way. About this, too, learned commentators still argue. Where
James is concerned, I am far from being a learned commentator;
and I have nothing to contribute to these traditional arguments
about *Varieties*. Instead I want to address a different question, one
that has attracted a lot less attention.

What difference did James's book make for the new discipline of
religious studies in the United States?

The least observant reader of *Varieties* will notice that the book
has nothing to do with comparative religion as its American scholars conceived their new field in 1902. First, the distinction between World Religions and more localized 'ethnic' or 'anthropological' religions was completely irrelevant to James. Second, James
equally ignored the paradigm of historical development from more

primitive to more sophisticated religions. Third, *Varieties* omitted the authoritative texts like the Bible that were of central concern to comparative religion. Fourth, James had no interest in comparing non-European religions to Christianity, the hobby-horse of many, perhaps most, learned students of religion. Indeed, although James distinguished two different religious *temperaments*, he did not compare any actual religions to each other. James's focus on the empirical data of unusual religious experiences took a psychological approach to religion that threw the canons of inquiry in the new discipline into the trash.

Yet James's originality in the new field of religious studies did not actually lie in his attention to psychology per se. Psychological accounts of religion long antedate the emergence of the discipline. One thinks of David Hume's "Natural History of Religion" (1757), where Hume explains the origin of belief in gods in "the incessant hopes and fears, which actuate the human mind" — or even of Statius's *Thebaid* written in the first century c.e.: "Fear first created gods in the world!" Early in the nineteenth century Friedrich Schleiermacher famously located the origin of religion in the human feeling of dependence. Psychological factors continued to play an important part in some later works now regarded as founding classics of the discipline — even in those of William Robertson Smith, who insisted that ritual practice trumped any mental elements in early religions. But Morris Jastrow insisted in 1911 that emotion predominated *only* in "the earliest forms of religion," while the balance shifted in favor of intellect as religions matured. As Crawford Toy observed the year before James began to lecture in Edinburgh, psychology treated the "starting-point of religion" rather than its matured development. Therefore psychology was marginal — or, more precisely, merely preparatory — to the *texts* that primarily concerned Toy's scholarly peers in religious studies.[25]

Toy's judgment was both right and wrong — right with respect to scholars of comparative religion, wrong with respect to a different discipline, the so-called New Psychology.[26] Toy probably did not regularly read the *American Journal of Psychology*. In that journal a couple of young psychologists, Edwin Starbuck (1866–1947) and James Leuba (1867–1946), began publishing in the mid-1890s research on the religious experiences of contemporary Americans. And these contemporary Americans typically adhered to exactly the sort of 'grown-up' World Religion that comparative-religion scholars studied: in this case Protestant Christianity. Starbuck did pioneering work using questionnaires to get data on personal religious experiences, from which he tried to generate empirical generalizations. Leuba also collected information in this way, but he strove to reduce religious experiences to physiological states, an American version of the German 'medical materialism' of the period. (Leuba is probably best remembered, if at all, for a 1916 poll of the religious beliefs of American scientists, meant to debunk Christianity.) Starbuck's and Leuba's early publications focused in particular on a widespread experience among American evangelical Protestants, conversion. In 1899 Starbuck published a book on the subject — with a preface by William James. Although Starbuck's book eventually came to be deemed a minor classic in religious studies, it took years to achieve this status, presumably because of the field's earlier focus on 'scriptures' rather than experience.[27]

James had learned of Starbuck's work when Starbuck studied at Harvard in 1893. At first skeptical of the younger man's questionnaires, in *Varieties* James made heavy use of data gleaned from them. Leuba, too, appeared in *Varieties*, albeit more briefly. James found him much less sympathetic; his tendency to materialist reductionism affronted James's radical empiricism and his sympathy for the pragmatic, personal truth of religious experience. *Varieties* also discussed a 1900 book dealing with conversion and based on similar empirical research by the Northwestern University psychologist George Coe. Nor did these studies exhaust the interest of the New Psychology in religion: the eminent G. Stanley Hall presided over a sort of 'school' of religious psychology at the new Clark University — a program whose best-known graduates were Leuba and Starbuck.[28]

Despite these psychologists of religion propagating like bunnies in the 1890s, Crawford Toy was correct *in a disciplinary sense* when he dismissed the importance of psychology to the study of religion. All of the aforementioned works on the psychology of religion seem to have flown beneath the radar of Toy's scholarly peers in comparative religion — until *after* the appearance of *Varieties*. And studies of personal religious experience began to appear *within the 'science of religion'* only several years after James published.[29] So James entered a peculiar situation when he stepped up to the podium in Edinburgh. Psychological research into religious experience, though a recent innovation, was well under way; but an unbridged gap yawned between it and the new academic discipline focused on the study of religions.

As it happened, the one major exception to Toy's generalization *within* the field was his own predecessor in teaching comparative religion at Harvard Divinity School, Carroll Everett. Before entering the Unitarian ministry, Everett had studied in Berlin in 1850–51 with Hegel's successor, Georg Andreas Gabler. Everett's intellectual loyalty thereafter remained fixed on Hegel, whose system "charmed me with its beauty and simplicity" — not, perhaps, the standard American response to reading Hegel. In 1869, while pastoring a church in Maine, Everett published a very Hegelian work on the logic of human thought. This book impressed the Harvard Corporation enough for it to offer Everett a chair in the Divinity School — though, oddly, a chair in New Testament criticism and interpretation: not exactly his long suit. Three years later

Everett took over James Freeman Clarke's course in comparative religion. Everett's version focused on the religions of eastern and southern Asia. One outgrowth of his teaching was a sixty-two-page pamphlet on pre-Christian religions intended as a textbook for Unitarian Sunday-school lessons on comparative religion. (In the spirit of Max Müller, the booklet included a chapter on ancient Aryan religion.) A more scholarly result was occasional articles by Everett concerning comparative religion in *The New World: A Quarterly Review of Religion, Ethics, and Theology*, for which journal Everett was lead editor from its founding in 1892 until his death in 1900.[30]

But Everett also taught, from 1870 until he died, a course on the psychology of religious faith, preparatory to a longer course on theology proper. Everett first called his psychology course "The Science of Religion" (parallel to his book *The Science of Thought*), then "The Psychological Basis of Religion," and finally "The Psychological Elements of Religious Faith." The substance, however, changed little, mostly the arrangement of the material varying. Despite his adulation of Hegel, Everett's lectures owed perhaps more to Friedrich Schleiermacher than to Schleiermacher's abusive enemy Hegel; but Everett's version of psychological idealism did not match very closely either of his German mentors' (whose differences he understood well). Everett agreed with Schleiermacher (and disagreed with Hegel) that "in religion feeling has the primacy as compared with intellect." But he rejected Schleiermacher's argument that religion springs from the human sense of dependency. Everett claimed instead that "the higher feelings imply a certain content in the divinity" and that this content consists of the traditional triad "truth, goodness, and beauty." Further details of Everett's psychology-of-religion course need not detain us. We need chiefly to register its existence; its old-fashioned speculative rather than empirical approach; its German idealist outlook, repugnant to William James; and its possible effect in stirring up James.[31]

For Carroll Everett personally was far from repugnant to James: he was a valued, older friend. In the 1870s and 1880s they had cheerfully sparred with each other: friendly foes in occasional informal clubs for philosophical discussion that sprang up in Cambridge like mushrooms after a rain and vanished as quickly. At least once Everett seems to have persuaded James publicly to backtrack on some philosophic issue (the details of this episode obscured by the mists of time). In the much smaller Harvard of those days, the two men would have continued to bump into each other often — maybe especially after 1889, when James moved into a new house only a few minutes' walk from the Divinity School. When Everett passed away, James's grief was probably not profound; but it was heartfelt.[32]

During the three decades when Everett was lecturing on the psychology of religion, James was himself grappling with the psychology of religion in a way far less abstract, much closer to home, and far less clearly defined.[33] William James's religious upbringing was, to say the least, atypical for prosperous Americans of his generation. His father, Henry James the elder, had struggled with his inherited Calvinism before finally settling into a rather eclectic Swedenborgianism a couple of years after William's birth in 1842. To comment that the religious situation in the James household remained fluid during William's growing-up is a massive understatement. Transcendentalists were one substantial presence there, with their questioning, uncertain version of Christianity or something beyond. Religion provided a frequent topic of discussion in the James household, but never of inculcation. Despite the omnipresence of religion in William James's earlier years — or because of it — he never affiliated with any religious group, rarely went to church, and never had a religious experience of the sort he later wrote about in *Varieties*.

He did come close. James suffered recurrent severe depression in the 1860s and 1870s. In *Varieties*, he described a nightmare hallucination followed by a terrifying "sense of the insecurity of life," allegedly reported to him by an unnamed "sufferer" writing in French. This episode was, James said, "like a revelation"; and he compared it explicitly to religious experiences of John Bunyan. Biographers, following speculation by William's son Harry after his father's death, have usually taken this account in *Varieties* as a disguised incident in James's own life, dating it to around 1870. This shattering episode "contributed to his understanding of religious mysticism," according to his student Ralph Barton Perry. Recently, the James scholar Paul Croce has argued persuasively that the case in *Varieties* is more likely "a composite of [James's] personal experiences, written from memory, and edited for public delivery and for illustration of psychological points about a religious type in the *Varieties*." Other, pleasanter "experiences that resembled mystical events," as Gerald Myers put it, may also have contributed to James's understanding of religious experience.[34]

But none of this made him a believer. Trained in chemistry, comparative anatomy, and medicine, James felt the tug of the scientific naturalism that seized the minds of a significant fraction of American intellectuals in the wake of Darwin; and this ruled out for him any firm belief in a God like the Christian one. Yet he did not go down the antireligion path of a contemporary like his friend Oliver Wendell Holmes Jr., whose agnosticism amounted in practice to atheism. James's own religious position is perhaps best described as a genuinely open-minded agnosticism, willing seriously to consider the possible reality of the supernatural. I once knew a dog, Mickey, whose owner said, "Mickey *wants* to be good; he just can't bring himself to do it." One might say something similar about James and religion. So *other* people's religious lives intrigued him; and, as his Harvard colleague George Herbert Palmer said, "To the last he kept ample room in his empiric universe for spiritual forces." Holmes was characteristically more acid: James, he said, kept "the lights down low so as to give miracle a chance."[35]

Yet during the 1870s and 1880s the lights in James's psychological laboratory shone brightly enough to keep his eyes focused on more mundane matters, and it was only after the publication of the *Principles of Psychology* in 1890 that James fixed his attention on the philosophic interests that he had long nurtured. Meanwhile, his annoyance mounted at what he saw as the narrow-minded exclusivity of scientific materialism, which dogmatically refused to admit the possibility of anything beyond the physical world. (James's aversion to "sectarian science" was of a piece with his well-known skepticism about the advance of disciplinary specialization in the university and its chopping up of knowledge into unconnected pieces.) James's most celebrated expression of this exasperation came in *The Varieties of Religious Experience* itself:

> I can, of course, put myself into the sectarian scientist's attitude, and imagine vividly that the world of sensations and scientific laws and objects may be all. But whenever I do this, I hear that inward monitor of which W. K. Clifford once wrote, whispering the word 'bosh!' Humbug is humbug, even though it bear the scientific name, and the total expression of human experience, as I view it objectively, invincibly urges me beyond the narrow 'scientific' bounds. Assuredly, the real world is of a different temperament — more intricately built than physical science allows.

But James's fretting about science's (or 'scientism's') narrowing of reality to the material world had become a settled worry years earlier; and by the later 1890s he was pouring more and more of his writing into "a defence of our right to adopt a believing attitude in religious matters," as he phrased the principle in his famous 1896 essay "The Will to Believe."[36]

This context helps to explain why James accepted the invitation to deliver the Gifford Lectures in Edinburgh in 1901 and 1902; and historians have advanced other motives for James's giving the lectures, such as filial piety toward his father's strong religiosity. But none of these motives tell us why James gave the lectures he did, as distinct from *some kind* of lectures on religion. That is, I am trying to explain not why James accepted the invitation to lecture on religion, but why the lectures took the form they did. The lectureship, after all, required its incumbents to address "natural theology"; and James's philosophizing on the right to believe probably came closer to natural theology than the "Study in Human Nature" that he actually produced. *Varieties* did owe a great deal to James's recent pragmatic turn in philosophy, being closely tied to and shaped by James's pragmatism; but my purpose here is to explicate the significance of *Varieties* within the context of American academic religious studies, not to explore James's philosophy.[37] And the book was neither philosophy nor natural theology in any conventional sense. I speculate that James had two principal reasons for doing as he did. The reason he gave at the beginning of the lectures — "psychology is the only branch of learning in which I am particularly versed"[38] — was probably not one of them. His real motives, I suspect, were dissatisfaction with *how* psychologists studied religion and his parallel dissatisfaction with the new academic discipline of religion.

His stated reason — that he himself was a psychologist — seems straightforward; but it is not. James certainly ranked among the world's most famous psychologists. But the text of *Varieties* leads me to believe that invoking this status was primarily a rhetorical strategy. He had, after all, been writing mostly philosophy for a decade. Merely mentioning that he was "versed" in psychology called attention to his reputation in the field. He thereby claimed the authority to judge the discipline — and to repudiate it as it actually practiced the study of religion. I invite you to compare *Varieties* both with other contemporary writings on the psychology of religion and with contemporary writings on comparative religion. I believe the two other motives I postulated then emerge from the text. Let us look at them in turn.

The first was James's dissatisfaction with psychological studies of religion. Psychology still came in two basic flavors in 1901. One was the traditional, introspective psychological speculation closely allied with philosophy — most famously, John Locke's *Essay Concerning Human Understanding*, which today we classify as philosophy rather than psychology. Within the universities this style of psychology had come to look musty and old-fashioned in James's day, but it still existed. One example was Carroll Everett's course at Harvard Divinity School on the psychology of religion. I do not know if James ever heard any of Everett's lectures; but he must have known of the course, given how long Everett taught it and how often he and James interacted intellectually in small, informal philosophic clubs in Cambridge. Fond as James was of Everett personally, Everett's course would have appalled him intellectually. First, because Everett's approach to psychology was abstracted from real human experience, it flew in the face of James's radical empiricism. Second, because Everett's philosophical psychology was heavily inflected by German idealism, it promoted the American neo-Hegelianism that was James's philosophical bête noire — and that he and Everett had personally sparred over. This is why I wonder if Everett's version of psychology of religion, well known around Harvard for decades, may have played some small part in stirring James to offer an alternative.

The so-called New Psychology was rapidly pushing philosophical psychology out of academic respectability. James himself had fostered this 'modern' competitor to philosophical psychology. But he nurtured growing doubts about the chick he had helped to hatch. The New Psychology was self-consciously scientific in method and ideology. It favored quantitative results and often employed laboratory experiments. James's great book *The Principles of Psychology* was, on one hand, the most important American exponent of the New Psychology and, on the other, a capaciously imagined effort to break out of its physiological straitjacket. Other New Psychologists adopted one of two approaches: either a monism that denied a spiritual world and limited reality to the material facts that science investigated, or a dualism that sharply distinguished nature from spirit. Idiosyncratically, James longed, in Paul Croce's words, "to find evidence for the operation of immaterial and spiritual elements within the natural."[39] Since publication of the *Principles* in 1890, James had grown more and more wary of the intellectual imperialism of naturalistic science in general and of physiological psychology in particular — that is, of the sweeping claim of many scientists that (in James's words) "the world of sensations and scientific laws and objects may be all." In the person of James Leuba, William James saw precisely a "sectarian scientific" program that tried to reduce human ideas and feelings — and specifically religious experiences — to physiological responses. But even Edwin Starbuck, from whom James borrowed much material, turned the richly lived human experiences he collected into quantitative generalizations. Perhaps George Coe stood closer intellectually to James than any other of these American psychologists; but Coe, too, looked with suspicion on the kind of mystical experiences in which James reveled and sought to relate them "to the recognized laws of the mental and bodily life" with "all the precision that modern psychological methods and tools render possible."[40] In *The Varieties of Religious Experience* James sought to reverse the scientistic tide of the New Psychology and recover the empirical diversity of real life. The book was, after all, not subtitled something like 'a psychological study.' It was subtitled *A Study in Human Nature.*

For, despite dressing himself up as a psychologist at the start of *Varieties*, James was not trying to bring the discipline of psychology into the new discipline of comparative religion. He was trying to warn students of religion away from it. Serious academic psychological studies of religion in 1902 would have meant fencing religious experience within the simplifying, reductionist categories of the laboratory or the scientific survey. James taught in *The Principles of Psychology* that sensory experience comes to us in a continuous, disorderly, undifferentiated flux of perceptions — a constantly flowing "stream of thought": what became famous in modernist fiction as the stream of consciousness. Consciousness for James was not a separate mental faculty but simply the preconscious decision to pay attention to, to focus on, some particular moment in this flux.[41] For this reason, the subconscious mind drew his strong interest; and from this preconscious swirl, he believed, came the mystical experiences he wrote about in *Varieties*.[42] To reduce them to neat categories or to physiological responses was to play false to their irreducibly individual character. James was far from hostile to science. But he feared that the hegemony of materialistic science was closing off human options. Hungry for a reality characterized by rampant individualism — what he called radical empiricism — he refused to give over all human experience to science as practiced circa 1900. He wished to foster a new science, with a broader vision of what 'reality' comprised.

And so James also wanted to shake up the academic study of religion by moving it away from what he saw as an already overly abstract, schematic approach, remote from human realities. This dissatisfaction was his second principal motive for structuring *Varieties* as he did. James had followed the scientific study of religion since its earliest days as a discipline. At the beginning of *Varieties*, James identified what he understood to be the currently dominant methods in what he, like Max Müller, called "the science of religions."

There were three: history of religions, theology, and anthropology. (It is a little surprising that he did not mention philology, notably Sanskrit philology.) All of these approaches stood aloof from real, lived religious experience. James revolted. He told his listeners (and readers) that he would ignore "religious institutions" (a term he meant inclusively, covering theological systems as well as churches). He offered instead a "descriptive survey" of "religious feelings and religious impulses." He also shifted the psychological focus away from early religions — where the new discipline had concentrated a lot of attention — to modern and even contemporary religious experience, which the student could get at more directly.[43]

In short, *The Varieties of Religious Experience* can best be seen, in the longer history of religious studies in the United States, as a strenuous effort at academic intellectual reform. James believed religion to be a vital aspect of human life. He thought it merited close study, and he wished for scholars (among others) to pay it more attention. He did not deny the value of research into the religious rituals and mythologies of tribal peoples, nor did he dispute the importance of learning about the ideas and institutions of the so-called World Religions. But he regarded the essential core of religion to lie in inner religious experiences — the ultimate source of and reason for, as he saw it, all religious thought and practice. He believed, rightly, that the new discipline of comparative religion almost totally neglected this foundation. By doing so, the scholars of religion abandoned this essential core of religion to the tender mercies of the science that officially dealt with inner experiences — psychology. The Old Psychology trafficked in philosophical abstraction, but it was on the way out, anyway. The New Psychology, James feared — again, rightly — would tend to reduce these complex, diverse, living experiences to mere physiology or dead, black-and-white generalizations. James tried to teach the young discipline of religious studies how to do a better job. He wanted a new "critical

Science of Religions," using as its experimental evidence, so to speak, the "facts of personal experience." ('Experience' and 'experiment,' after all, used to mean the same thing.) He believed such a science might "eventually command" the same degree of public assent "as is commanded by a physical science."[44] That last hope, needless to say, was a pipe dream.

Did he otherwise succeed? Inevitably, the answer is yes and no — or, more accurately, first no and then yes. Immediately on publication *The Varieties of Religious Experience* was recognized as a major work, almost an instant classic. Many reviewers doubted the plausibility of explaining religious experience on the basis of what James admitted to be its "extremer expressions." But almost no one doubted the quality or importance of the book. And so *Varieties* became an enduring presence in religious studies.

And yet for decades it stood as a solitary pillar around which professors tilling the field of religious studies did everything but imitate it. Some psychologists continued to investigate religion — usually in ways that would have made James wince. In 1904, G. Stanley Hall launched *The American Journal of Religious Psychology and Education*, abetted by Coe, Leuba, and Starbuck among others; it lasted for over a decade.[45] But the professional students of comparative religion neglected James's version of religious experience. This hardly comes as a shock. After all, James's *Varieties* flouted the great European philological and sociological models of research into religion. Perhaps more important, his approach could say nothing about how Christianity stood in relation to other religions — still the burning question for most American religious-studies scholars during the first half of the twentieth century. After all, the major organization for academic students of religion in America, founded in 1909, was the National Association of Biblical Instructors.[46] Only in 1964 did the association rename itself the American Academy of Religion.

This change of name reflected a great expansion of religious studies in American universities after World War II. With this growth in numbers came a broadening of interests, and in this new environment William James became for the first time really relevant to the discipline. Long recognized as a classic, *Varieties* now became something of a model. To be sure, the great majority of scholars of religion today study religions in ways far different from James, but many religious-studies experts do follow a Jamesian path to understanding religious experience. And without *Varieties* in the background, it is hard to believe that we would today enjoy such a rich, well, variety of studies as Wayne Proudfoot's *Religious Experience*, Richard Rabinowitz's *The Spiritual Self in Everyday Life*, and Ann Taves's *Fits, Trances, and Visions.*[47] In this sense James eventually won. He stretched the map of religious studies in America.

NOTES

CHAPTER ONE. The Dog That Didn't Bark

1. For the entrance of the humanities into American higher education, see Jon H. Roberts and James Turner, *The Sacred and the Secular University*, part 2 (Princeton: Princeton University Press, 2000); Caroline Winterer, *The Culture of Classicism: Ancient Greece and Rome in American Intellectual Life, 1780–1910* (Baltimore: Johns Hopkins University Press, 2002); and Laurence Veysey's aging, flawed, but still cogent essay "The Plural Organized Worlds of the Humanities," in *The Organization of Knowledge in Modern America, 1860–1920*, ed. Alexandra Oleson and John Voss (Baltimore: Johns Hopkins University Press, 1979), 51–106.

2. Biological anthropology, archaeology, and linguistic anthropology are different cases.

3. On the contrast between pagan and Christian attitudes, see Eric J. Sharpe, *Comparative Religion: A History*, 2nd ed. (LaSalle, Ill.: Open Court, 1986), 2–10.

4. In full: "I am the LORD thy God, which have brought thee out of the land of Egypt, out of the house of bondage. Thou shalt have no other gods before me." Exodus 20: 2–3, King James Version. Christian groups differ on whether the first sentence (verse 2) forms an integral part of the First Commandment, as distinct from a sort of preface to the commandments as a whole. All, I believe, include the second sentence (verse 3).

5. Recent examples, differing sharply in temperament and point of view but largely agreeing on the broad outlines of the story, are Sharpe, *Comparative Religion*; Hans G. Kippenberg, *Die Entdeckung der Religionsgeschichte: Religionswissenschaft und Moderne* (München: Verlag

C.H. Beck, 1997); Tomoko Masuzawa, *The Invention of World Religions; or, How European Universalism Was Preserved in the Language of Pluralism* (Chicago: University of Chicago Press, 2005). Princeton University Press published an English version of Kippenberg in 2002 (trans. Barbara Harshav) under the slightly bleached title *Discovering Religious History in the Modern Age*. One can see this standard narrative already taking shape over a century ago in Louis Henry Jordan, *Comparative Religion: Its Genesis and Growth* (Edinburgh: T. & T. Clark, 1905). H. Pinard de la Boullaye, S.J., *L'Étude comparée des religions*, 2 vols. (Paris: G. Beauchesne, 1929), unusually took a broader view of the development of the discipline in his first, historical volume. Walter H. Capps, *Religious Studies: The Making of a Discipline* (Minneapolis: Fortress Press, 1995), is a methodological argument using historical materials rather than a history of the field.

6. Survey data from 2008 show a majority of Americans believing that a non-Christian religion can lead to eternal life. To say that, for example, a Muslim can attain eternal life is not the same as agreeing that Islam is true or even partly true. Still, the percentage of Americans who affirmed that "Mine is the one true faith" ranged from only 49 percent even among white evangelicals to a mere 11 percent among white Catholics. "Many Americans Say Other Faiths Can Lead to Eternal Life," Pew Forum on Religion and Public Life, December 18, 2008, http://pewforum.org/docs/?DocID=380, accessed October 20, 2009.

7. The most learned study of any of these episodes is Sabine MacCormack, *Religion in the Andes: Vision and Imagination in Early Colonial Peru* (Princeton: Princeton University Press, 1991).

8. William Robertson Smith, *Religion of the Semites* (1894; New Brunswick, N.J.: Transaction Publishers, 2002), xliv; Francis Schmidt, "Des inepties tolérable: la raison des rites de John Spencer à W. Robertson Smith," *Archives des sciences sociales de religions* 85 (1994): 132–33.

9. Jean-Luc Kieffer, *Anquetil-Duperron: l'Inde en France au XVIIIe siècle* (Paris: Les Belles Lettres, 1983). On Jones, see especially Garland Cannon, *The Life and Mind of Oriental Jones: Sir William Jones, the Father of Modern Linguistics* (Cambridge: Cambridge University Press, 1990);

S. N. Mukherjee, *Sir William Jones: A Study in Eighteenth-Century Attitudes to India* (Cambridge: Cambridge University Press, 1968); and Rosane Rocher, "Weaving Knowledge: Sir William Jones and Indian Pandits," in *Objects of Inquiry: The Life, Contributions, and Influences of Sir William Jones (1746–1794)*, ed. Garland Cannon and Kevin R. Brine (New York: New York University Press, 1995), 54–67. On British orientalist scholarship in this period more generally, see especially Thomas R. Trautmann, *Aryans and British India* (Berkeley and Los Angeles: University of California Press, 1997), and idem, *Languages and Nations: The Dravidian Proof in Colonial Madras* (Berkeley and Los Angeles: University of California Press, 2006). The classic and still indispensable starting point for the European intellectual 'discovery' of India is Raymond Schwab, *La Renaissance orientale* (Paris: Payot, 1950).

10. The date is a bit arbitrary. Müller had earlier devoted the first volume of his collected essays, *Chips from a German Workshop* (1867), to what he called "the science of religion." Crawford Toy took 1867 as the year in which the new discipline was "first formally introduced to the world." C. H. Toy, "Recent Work in the Science of Religion," *International Monthly* 1 (1900): 218. Morris Jastrow Jr., *The Study of Religion* (London: Walter Scott Publishing Co., 1911), 44, pointed to the 1870 lectures as the key moment.

11. Masuzawa, *Invention of World Religions*, 108, gives the year as 1873. This was actually when Tiele was appointed to the faculty of the Remonstrant seminary, newly moved to the city of Leiden.

12. Clarke gets space in Masuzawa, Sharpe, and Jordan, though not in Kippenberg. Sharpe, *Comparative Religion*, 97 (emphasis in original); Sydney E. Ahlstrom, *The American Protestant Encounter with World Religions*, the Brewer Lectures on Comparative Religion (Beloit, Wisc.: Beloit College, 1962), [4]n (unpaginated).

13. The only history of the field in the United States starts with the early days of university-based religious studies; that is, with the object of investigation already in place. Cf. Robert S. Shepard, *God's People in the Ivory Tower: Religion in the Early American University* (New York: Carlson Publishing, 1991).

14. For a recent expression of this point of view, see Timothy Fitzgerald, *The Ideology of Religious Studies* (New York: Oxford University Press, 2000).

15. David Abulafia, *The Discovery of Mankind: Atlantic Encounters in the Age of Columbus* (New Haven: Yale University Press, 2008), 130–44, 206.

16. Ibid., 47, 113, 155.

17. Ibid., 61, 222, 288, 292. Quotation from Juan López de Palacios Rubios, ca. 1513, on p. 292. Abulafia mentions that Gama's men noted the several arms of the god/saints but not the sailors' reaction.

18. The word "fetish" was used in English as early as the seventeenth century but did not receive serious analytic development until the nineteenth.

19. David Murray, "Spreading the Word: Missionaries, Conversion and Circulation in the Northeast," in *Spiritual Encounters: Interactions between Christianity and Native Religions in Colonial America*, ed. Nicholas Griffiths and Fernando Cervantes (Lincoln: University of Nebraska Press, 1999), 49–50.

20. Victor Egon Hanzeli, *Missionary Linguistics in New France: A Study of Seventeenth- and Eighteenth-Century Descriptions of American Indian Languages* (The Hague: Mouton, 1969), 17, 19–20, 22, 59, 64, 72–81.

21. Edward G. Gray, *New World Babel: Languages and Nations in Early America* (Princeton: Princeton University Press, 1999), 24–26, 44–50.

22. Murray, "Spreading the Word," 48–49.

23. [Benjamin Franklin], "The Captivity of William Henry," in *The Papers of Benjamin Franklin*, ed. Leonard W. Labaree et al. (New Haven: Yale University Press, 1959–), 15: 145–57. One cannot take this piece, originally published in the *London Chronicle*, June 23–25, 25–28, 1768, too seriously, since it was a hoax.

24. For important early instances, see Henry Rowe Schoolcraft, *Algic Researches, comprising Inquiries Respecting the Mental Characteristics of the North American Indians*, 2 vols. (New York: Harper & Brothers, 1839), a collection of "oral imaginative tales" (12); E. G. Squier, *The Serpent Symbol, and the Worship of the Reciprocal Principles of Nature in America* (New

York: G. P. Putnam, 1851), a more analytic study of widespread themes. Although Schoolcraft uses the word "mythology," it is not clear whether he regarded any Indian myths as an aspect of something that could be called religion.

25. Basil Willey, *The Seventeenth Century Background: Studies in the Thought of the Age in Relation to Poetry and Religion* (1934; New York: Columbia University Press, 1967), 123.

26. Marcus Tullius Cicero, *On the Commonwealth and on the Laws*, ed. James E. G. Zetzel (Cambridge: Cambridge University Press, 1999), 114 (*De legibus*, 1.24).

27. Willard, *A Compleat Body of Divinity in Two Hundred and Fifty Expository Lectures on the [Westminster] Assembly's Shorter Catechism* [Boston: B. Green and S. Kneeland, 1726], 37–40, 109, quoted in E. Brooks Holifield, *Theology in America: Christian Thought from the Age of the Puritans to the Civil War* (New Haven: Yale University Press, 2003), 71. Cf. Increase Mather, *A Discourse Proving that the Christian Religion is the Only True Religion: Wherein the Necessity of Divine Revelation is Evinced, in Several Sermons* (Boston: T. Green, 1702); Cotton Mather, *A Man of Reason* (Boston: John Edwards, 1718); and Cotton Mather, *Reason Satisfied: and Faith Established* (Boston: J. Allen, 1712).

28. This is more or less the argument of both Peter Byrne, *Natural Religion and the Nature of Religion: The Legacy of Deism* (London: Routledge, 1989), and Peter Harrison, *'Religion' and the Religions in the English Enlightenment* (Cambridge: Cambridge University Press, 1990), although I take full credit for the altar. As to the *origin* of the matured notion of 'religion' (as a genus of which many species exist, potentially subject to study both as a genus and by comparing species), I find more plausible the argument of Jonathan Sheehan, "Sacred and Profane: Idolatry, Antiquarianism and the Polemics of Distinction in the Seventeenth Century," *Past & Present* 192 (August 2006): 35–66. But the 'deist controversy' of the early 1700s did widely publicize natural religion in the anglophone world and praise it as an actually existing phenomenon and an alternative to Christianity — thus inspiring argument about what, e.g., the Chinese really did believe. I think it fair therefore to agree with Byrne

and Harrison that deism did to an unprecedented extent *popularize* in the English-speaking world the idea of religion as a general category for inquiry.

29. Michael Hunter, "'Aikenhead the Atheist': The Context and Consequences of Articulate Irreligion in the Late 17th Century," in Hunter, *Science and the Shape of Orthodoxy: Intellectual Change in Late Seventeenth-Century Britain* (Rochester, N.Y.: Boydell Press, 1995), 308–32.

30. The fullest account of the deist controversy remains the first volume of Leslie Stephen, *History of English Thought in the Eighteenth Century*, 3rd ed., 2 vols. (1902; New York: Harbinger Books — Harcourt, Brace & World, 1962). In more recent literature, see especially Robert E. Sullivan, *John Toland and the Deist Controversy: A Study in Adaptations* (Cambridge, Mass.: Harvard University Press, 1982); Wayne Hudson, *The English Deists: Studies in Early Enlightenment* (London: Pickering & Chatto, 2009); and Margaret C. Jacob, *The Radical Enlightenment: Pantheists, Freemasons, and Republicans* (London: Allen & Unwin, 1981). For the larger intellectual context, see Jonathan Israel's controversial two volumes, *Radical Enlightenment: Philosophy and the Making of Modernity, 1650–1750* (Oxford: Oxford University Press, 2001), and *Enlightenment Contested: Philosophy, Modernity, and the Emancipation of Man, 1670–1752* (Oxford: Oxford University Press, 2006).

31. For his distinctive polytheistic version of deism, see Benjamin Franklin, "Articles of Belief and Acts of Religion," manuscript dated November 20, 1728, in *The Papers of Benjamin Franklin*, ed. Leonard W. Labaree et al. (New Haven: Yale University Press, 1959–), 1: 102–3. For two opposed understandings of Franklin's beliefs, see Alfred Owen Aldridge, *Benjamin Franklin and Nature's God* (Durham, N.C.: Duke University Press, 1967), and Kerry S. Walters, *Benjamin Franklin and His Gods* (Urbana: University of Illinois Press, 1999). Walters has read widely in Franklin's writings, but Aldridge has a firmer grasp of the eighteenth-century context.

32. Kerry S. Walters, *Rational Infidels: The American Deists* (Durango, Colo.: Longwood Academic, 1992); G. Adolf Koch, *Republican Religion: The American Revolution and the Cult of Reason* (New York: Henry Holt

and Co., 1933); Herbert Morais, *Deism in Eighteenth-Century America* (New York: Columbia University Press, 1934); David L. Holmes, *The Religion of the Founding Fathers* (Charlottesville, Va.: Ash Lawn-Highland; Ann Arbor: Clements Library, University of Michigan, 2003).

33. Toland quoted in Sullivan, *Toland*, 185; [Arthur Bury], *The Naked Gospel* (n.p. [Oxford], 1690), preface [unpaginated], 2nd and 4th pages; [Matthew Tindal], *Christianity as Old as the Creation: or, the Gospel, a Republication of the Religion of Nature*, vol. 1 (London, 1730), 309–10 (quotation at 310; volume 2 was never published; the anonymity of both author and printer is not surprising in a work possibly subject to prosecution); Aldridge, *Franklin and Nature's God*, 120–21; Aldridge, *The Dragon and the Eagle: The Presence of China in the American Enlightenment* (Detroit: Wayne State University Press, 1993), 23–26.

34. Paolo Rossi, *The Dark Abyss of Time: The History of the Earth and the History of Nations from Hooke to Vico*, trans. Lydia G. Cochrane (1979; Chicago: University of Chicago Press, 1984), 129–32, 244; [Thomas Blackwell], *Letters Concerning Mythology* (London: n.p., 1748), letter 18, esp. 345, 349–50, 352–62; Frank E. Manuel, *The Eighteenth Century Confronts the Gods* (Cambridge, Mass.: Harvard University Press, 1959). My allusion to earlier researches is to John Spencer; see above. Blackwell's anonymous publication signifies nothing; he had a penchant for a pretense of anonymity.

35. Michael J. Lee, *American Revelations: Biblical Interpretation and Criticism in America, circa 1700–1860* (PhD diss., University of Notre Dame, 2009), chap. 1; Mather, *American Tears upon the Ruins of the Greek Churches* (Boston, 1701), 46, and *Manuductio ad Ministerium* (Boston, 1726), 93–94, quoted in Richard F. Lovelace, *The American Pietism of Cotton Mather* (Grand Rapids, Mich.: Christian University Press, 1979), 42 and 47; Gerald R. McDermott, *Jonathan Edwards Confronts the Gods: Christian Theology, Enlightenment Religion, and Non-Christian Faiths* (New York: Oxford University Press, 2000), 6; Carl T. Jackson, *The Oriental Religions and American Thought: Nineteenth-Century Explorations* (Westport, Conn.: Greenwood Press, 1981), 3–4.

36. This paragraph and the next rely on McDermott, *Edwards Confronts the Gods*, for information about Edwards, but McDermott should not be blamed for my interpretation of the larger context.

37. Aldridge, *Dragon and Eagle*, 23–24.

38. Stewart, "Account of the Life and Writings of Adam Smith LLD," in Smith, *Essays on Philosophical Subjects*, Glasgow Edition of the Works and Correspondence of Adam Smith, vol. 3, ed. W. P. D. Wightman, J. C. Bryce, and I. S. Ross (1795; Indianapolis: Liberty Classics, 1982), 293.

39. In a vast and growing literature, the starting point remains Henry F. May, *The Enlightenment in America* (New York: Oxford University Press, 1976).

40. Thomas Jefferson, *Notes on the State of Virginia* [1787], ed. William Peden (1954; New York: W. W. Norton & Co., 1972), 101.

41. Louise Chipley, "The Enlightenment Library of William Bentley," *Essex Institute Historical Collections* 122 (1986): 3 (and 3n3), 4–5, 11; entry for May 2, 1794, in *The Diary of William Bentley, D.D., Pastor of the East Church, Salem, Massachusetts*, 4 vols. (1905; Gloucester, Mass.: Peter Smith, 1962), 2: 88.

42. A search of the Rotunda digital edition of *The Papers of Thomas Jefferson*, ed. Barbara B. Oberg and J. Jefferson Looney, gives this null result (http://p8080-rotunda.upress.virginia.edu.proxy.library.nd.edu/founders/default.xqy?keys=TSJN-info-search, accessed December 1, 2009). The handful of allusions by Jefferson to "Mahometan" or "Hindoo" are purely rhetorical and curt.

43. Manuel, *Eighteenth Century Confronts Gods*, 271–80; Jackson, *Oriental Religions*, 30–31.

44. *A Comparison of the Institutions of Moses with Those of the Hindoos and Other Ancient Nations; with Remarks on Mr. Dupuis's Origin of All Religions, the Laws and Institutions of Moses Methodized, and an Address to the Jews on the Present State of the World and the Prophecies Relating to It* (Northumberland, Pa.: Printed for the author by A. Kennedy, 1799).

45. Joseph Priestley, *Discourses Relating to the Evidence of Revealed Religion: Delivered in the Church of the Universalists, at Philadelphia, 1796; and Published at the Request of Many of the Hearers* (Philadelphia:

Printed for T. Dobson, by John Thompson, 1796), and *Discourses Relating to the Evidences of Revealed Religion, Delivered in Philadelphia*, vol. 2 (Philadelphia: Printed by Thomas Dobson, 1797). (The first of these titles bears no volume number.) In the 1796 discourses, Priestley devoted a chapter to comparisons with "Heathen Philosophy," in the 1797 discourses a chapter to comparisons with "Mahametanism."

46. Priestley, *Comparison of the Institutions*, sections [chap.] 7 and 8.

47. Aldridge, *Dragon and Eagle*, 93.

48. May, *Enlightenment in America*.

49. Amasa Delano, *Narrative of Voyages and Travels, in the Northern and Southern Hemispheres: Comprising Three Voyages Round the World; Together with a Voyage of Survey and Discovery, in the Pacific Ocean and Oriental Islands*, 2nd ed. (Boston: Printed by E. G. House, for the Author, 1818), 71, 160, 230, 242–46, 533–35.

50. Trautmann, *Aryans and British India*; Philip C. Almond, *The British Discovery of Buddhism* (Cambridge: Cambridge University Press, 1988); Jackson, *Oriental Religions*, 5–6; Aldridge, *Dragon and Eagle*, 192–94, 196–97, 206–9, 264–65. Aldridge points out that only half of Waln's book made it into print; the rest survives in manuscript in the Library Company of Philadelphia.

51. Nancy F. Cott, *The Bonds of Womanhood: "Women's Sphere" in New England, 1780–1835* (New Haven: Yale University Press, 1977), 7.

52. Biographical information is drawn from Hannah Adams [and Hannah Farnham Sawyer Lee], *A Memoir of Miss Hannah Adams, Written by Herself. With Additional Notices, by a Friend* (Boston: Gray and Bowen, 1832). All my quotations come from the first forty-three pages, the portion written by Adams herself.

53. Adams [and Lee], *Memoir*, 1–3, 8, 10. Thomas A. Tweed, "An American Pioneer in the Study of Religion: Hannah Adams (1755–1831) and Her 'Dictionary of All Religions,'" *Journal of the American Academy of Religions* 60 (1992): 446, implies that the boarder had the entire book to show Adams. This contradicts her own clear statement.

54. Thomas Broughton, *An Historical Dictionary of All Religions from the Creation of the World to This Present Time . . . Compiled from the Best*

Authorities, 2 vols. (London: Printed for C. Davis; and T. Harris, 1742), 2: 20.

55. The manuscript extract that Adams saw compared only "Arminians, Calvinists, and several other [Christian] denominations which were most common." Adams [and Lee], *Memoir*, 10. The Unitarian-Trinitarian war originated as a dispute between Arminians and Calvinists.

56. Adams [and Lee], *Memoir*, 11, 14, 22, 43.

57. Hannah Adams, *An Alphabetical Compendium of the Various Sects Which Have Appeared in the World from the Beginning of the Christian Æra to the Present Day: With an Appendix, Containing a Brief Account of the Different Schemes of Religion Now Embraced among Mankind: The Whole Collected from the Best Authors, Ancient and Modern* (Boston: Printed by B. Edes & Sons, 1784).

58. Hannah Adams, *A View of Religions, in Two Parts. Part I. Containing an Alphabetical Compendium of the Various Religious Denominations, Which Have Appeared in the World, from the Beginning of the Christian Era to the Present Day. Part II. Containing a Brief Account of the Different Schemes of Religion Now Embraced Among Mankind. The Whole Collected from the Best Authors, Ancient and Modern* (Boston: Printed by John West Folsom, 1791).

59. With the same title as the 1791 edition, but now "Printed by and for Manning & Loring" of Boston.

60. Hannah Adams, *A Dictionary of All Religions and Religious Denominations, Jewish, Heathen, Mahometan, and Christian, Ancient and Modern. With an Appendix, Containing a Sketch of the Present State of the World, as to Population, Religion, Toleration, Missions, Etc. and the Articles in Which All Christian Denominations Agree* (New York: James Eastburn and Company, and Boston: Cummings and Hilliard, 1817).

61. Adams [and Lee], *Memoir*, 38–39.

62. Adams, *Alphabetical Compendium*, "Advertisement" (unnumbered page in front matter), "Appendix," iv-xvii.

63. E.g., Jackson, *Oriental Religions*, 16–19; Masuzawa, *Invention of World Religions*, 58–59.

64. Adams, *Alphabetical Compendium*, "Appendix," [i]–ii, iv–xvii, xl–xli, xliii–xlv, xlviii, lv–lvi, lix–lx, lxv–lxvii, lxx, lxxii, lxxvii–lxxviii. In keeping with western usage at the time, Adams called the Dalai Lama the Grand Lama.

65. Adams, *View of Religions* (1791), 343–44, 349; Aldridge, *Dragon and Eagle*, 43–44; *A Code of Gentoo Laws, or Ordinations of the Pundits, from a Persian Translation, Made from the Original, Written in the Shanscrit Language*, trans. Nathaniel Brassey Halhed (London: [East India Company], 1776); *The Bhagvat-geeta, or Dialogues of Kreeshna and Arjoon*, trans. Charles Wilkins (1785; Gainesville, Fla.: Scholars' Facsimiles & Reprints, 1959).

66. Adams, *View of Religions* (1801), 313, 405ff.; Trautmann, *Aryans*, 75. Maurice's work, published between 1793 and 1800, was *Indian Antiquities: or, Dissertations, relative to the Ancient Geographical Divisions, the Pure System of Primeval Theology, the Grand Code of Civil Laws, the Original Form of Government, and the Various and Profound Literature of Hindostan*.

67. Adams, *Dictionary of All Religions*, preface (unnumbered page).

68. Jordan, *Comparative Religion*, 146–49.

CHAPTER TWO. Comparing Religions in an
Age of Uncertainty, circa 1820 to 1875

1. James C. Moffat, *Biblical Criticism as an Object of Popular Interest: An Address Delivered at the Opening of the Third Session of the Cincinnati Theological Seminary of the Presbyterian Church* (Cincinnati: John D. Thorpe, 1852), 15–16.

2. Carl T. Jackson, *The Oriental Religions and American Thought: Nineteenth-Century Explorations* (Westport, Conn.: Greenwood Press, 1981), chap. 5.

3. *All Religions and Religious Ceremonies: In Two Parts. Part I. Christianity-Mahometanism, and Judaism. . . . Part II. A View of the History-Religion-Manners and Customs of the Hindoos. By William Ward. Together with the Religion and Ceremonies of Other Pagan Nations* (Hartford,

Conn.: Oliver D. Cooke & Sons, 1823); *A View, of the History, Literature, and Religion, of the Hindoos: Including a Minute Description of Their Manners and Customs . . . from the Second Edition, Carefully Abridged, and Greatly Improved* (Hartford, Conn.: H. Huntington, Jr., 1824); Charles A. Goodrich, *A Pictorial and Descriptive View of All Religions; Embracing the Forms of Worship Practiced by the Several Nations of the Known World, from the Earliest Records to the Present Time* (Hartford, Conn.: Sumner and Goodman, 1842), quotations at 5–6, 15. So far as I can determine, Goodrich's book began its American life as *Religious Ceremonies and Customs, or the Forms of Worship Practiced by the Several Nations of the Known World, from the Earliest Records to the Present Time* (Hartford, Conn.: Hutchinson and Dwier, 1834). I have no idea why Hartford became the entrepot of such works, but New England was the heartland of American missionary efforts in Asia, while its merchants (see below) traded to India and China.

4. *The Monthly Anthology* 2 (1805): 360–66, 370–76. For the culture, including religion, of the New England mercantile elite, see James Turner, *The Liberal Education of Charles Eliot Norton* (Baltimore: Johns Hopkins University Press, 1999), prologue.

5. [Andrews Norton], "Notice of Eminent Individuals Lately Deceased: Rammohun Roy," *Select Journal of Foreign Periodical Literature* 3 (1834): 111; J. T., "Is Rammohun Roy a Christian? or, in Other Words, Is He a Believer in the Divine Authority of Our Lord?" *Christian Examiner and Theological Review*, 3 (1826): 361–69. Jackson, *Oriental Religions*, 32–36, provides a compact summary of Rammohan Roy and his impact on New England Unitarians (Rammohun, as Jackson and his sources spelled it; the name is spelled variously). For Rammohan's life and his Indian context, see B. C. Robertson, *Raja Rammohan Roy, the Father of Modern India* (Delhi: Oxford University Press, 1995); C. A. Bayly, "Rammohan Roy and the Advent of Constitutional Liberalism in India, 1800–1830," *Modern Intellectual History* 4 (2007): 25–41; and David Kopf, *British Orientalism and the Bengal Renaissance: The Dynamics of Indian Modernization, 1773–1835* (Berkeley and Los Angeles: University of California Press, 1969).

NOTES TO CHAPTER TWO

6. Jogendra Chunder Ghose and Eshan Chunder Bose, eds., *The English Works of Raja Rammohun Roy, with an English Translation of "Tuhfatul Muwahhiddin"* (Allahabad: Panini Office, 1906); [William Tudor], "Theology of Hindoos as taught by Ram Mohun Roy," *North American Review* 6 (1818): 386–93; "Religious Intelligence: A Remarkable Hindoo Reformer," *Christian Disciple* 5 (1817): 123–25; H. T., "Religious Intelligence: Rammohun Roy," *Christian Register* 1 (1821): [64] (December 7, 1821); Garland Cannon, *The Life and Mind of Oriental Jones: Sir William Jones, the Father of Modern Linguistics* (Cambridge: Cambridge University Press, 1990), 328. The collection of eighteen tracts by Rammohan bound together in the Harvard College Library (Ind 2014.1.5), which Harvard acquired in the 1840s (presumably by donation or bequest), suggests that his works circulated among Boston's Unitarian elite.

7. Elisabeth Hurth, *Between Faith and Unbelief: American Transcendentalists and the Challenge of Atheism* (Leiden: Brill, 2007), 193; Thomas A. Tweed, *The American Encounter with Buddhism, 1844–1912: Victorian Culture and the Limits of Dissent* (Bloomington: Indiana University Press, 1992), xviii; Philip C. Almond, *The British Discovery of Buddhism* (Cambridge: Cambridge University Press, 1988), chap. 1; [Edward Elbridge Salisbury?] "Buddhism," *New Englander and Yale Review* 3 (1845): 182–92; James Turner, *Without God, Without Creed: The Origins of Unbelief in America* (Baltimore: Johns Hopkins University Press, 1985), 154. I attribute the anonymous "Buddhism" article to Salisbury, the first important American orientalist, because (a) he taught at Yale, the *New Englander*'s base; (b) he knew the scant European scholarship on Buddhism better than any other American; and (c) he published on the subject in the *Journal of the American Oriental Society* 1 (1843–49): 79–135 and 275–98. Salisbury had studied with Burnouf.

8. *The Dial: A Magazine for Literature, Philosophy, and Religion* 3 (1842–43): 82–85, 331–40, 493–94; 4 (1843–44): 59–62, 205–10, 391–404, 529–36; Jackson, *Oriental Religions*, 59, 107; Arthur Versluis, *American Transcendentalism and Asian Religions* (New York: Oxford University Press, 1993), 284–86. On *Sacred Books of the East* see below.

9. Much of this sentence is borrowed from Turner, *Without God*, 165.

10. Ralph Waldo Emerson, "The Lord's Supper," in *The Selected Writings of Ralph Waldo Emerson*, ed. Brooks Atkinson (1940; New York: Modern Library, 1968), 116, 118.

11. Ralph Waldo Emerson, "Religion" [May 1867], in *Sketches and Reminiscences of the Radical Club of Chestnut Street, Boston*, ed. Mrs. John T. [Mary Elizabeth Fiske] Sargent (Boston: James R. Osgood and Company, 1880), 3–4, 6; Theodore Parker, *A Discourse of Matters Pertaining to Religion*, in *The Works of Theodore Parker*, centenary edition, 14 vols. (Boston: American Unitarian Association, 1907–11), 1: 35n, quoted in Jackson, *Oriental Religions*, 75.

12. Jackson, *Oriental Religions*, 66.

13. "A Discourse of the Transient and Permanent in Christianity" is reprinted in, e.g., Perry Miller, ed., *The Transcendentalists: An Anthology* (Cambridge, Mass.: Harvard University Press, 1967), 260–83.

14. Jackson, *Oriental Religions*, 51, 53, 56–57.

15. Jackson, *Oriental Religions*, 73–79.

16. A brief account of the founding appears in *Journal of the American Oriental Society* 1 (1843–49): ii.

17. This was true at least up to the early 1870s; I have not systematically studied the *Journal* afterwards.

18. Jackson, *Oriental Religions*, 96–99.

19. Thomas Wentworth Higginson, *The Sympathy of Religions*, Free Religious Tracts no. 3, new ed., rev. and enl. (1871; Boston: Free Religious Association, 1876), "Preliminary Note." The FRA's members included also liberal Jewish leaders and non-Unitarian freethinkers. Stow Persons, *Free Religion: An American Faith* (New Haven: Yale University Press, 1947); Jackson, *Oriental Religions*, chap. 6, studies specifically the FRA's interest in Asian religions.

20. Higginson, *Sympathy of Religions*, 5, 6, 8, 33. "The luxury of a religion that does not degrade" came from a speech that Emerson delivered to the 1869 meeting of the FRA, the Boston organization that published Higginson's tract. Higginson did not identify the source, possibly believing that readers would recognize the line. One finds an argument essentially similar to Higginson's in Samuel Longfellow, "The Unity and Universality

of the Religious Ideas," *The Radical* 3 (1868): 433–57. Longfellow, too, fits the profile of a Unitarian influenced by Transcendentalism.

21. Lydia Maria Child, *The Progress of Religious Ideas, through Successive Ages*, 3 vols. (New York: C. S. Francis and Co., 1855).

22. It is not even mentioned in the text of the article about her in the *American National Biography*, although the book does appear in the bibliography of the article.

23. Child, *Progress of Religious Ideas*, 1: ix. She lists her sources at 3: 463–64. For an assessment of her work and its relation to the Transcendentalists, see Versluis, *American Transcendentalism*, 236–42. (Versluis shares my low opinion of Child's scholarship but objects to my having called her book, in my *Without God, Without Creed*, "a mere 'pabulum.'" 'Mere' is Versluis's word, not mine; and I think he is confusing 'pabulum' with 'pablum.')

24. Child, *Progress of Religious Ideas*, 1: vii, viii, x.

25. Child, *Progress of Religious Ideas*, 1: viii; Jackson, *Oriental Religions*, 71; James Turner, "Religion et langage dans l'Amerique du XIXème siècle: le cas étrange de Andrews Norton," *Revue de l'histoire des religions* 210, no. 4 (1993): 431–62; idem, "Charles Hodge in the Intellectual Weather of the Nineteenth Century," in *Charles Hodge Revisited: A Critical Appraisal of His Life and Work,* ed. John W. Stewart and James H. Moorhead (Grand Rapids, Mich.: William B. Eerdmanns Publishing Co., 2002), 41–61.

26. Child, *Progress of Religious Ideas*, 3: 418–61.

27. Robert Lamberton, *Homer the Theologian: Neoplatonist Allegorical Reading and the Growth of the Epic Tradition* (Berkeley and Los Angeles: University of California Press, 1986), 10–15 and passim. One biblical critic argues that New Testament authors imitated Homer: Dennis R. MacDonald, *The Homeric Epics and the Gospel of Mark* (New Haven: Yale University Press, 2000), and *Does the New Testament Imitate Homer? Four Cases from the Acts of the Apostles* (New Haven: Yale University Press, 2003).

28. Conrad Cherry, *Hurrying toward Zion: Universities, Divinity Schools, and American Protestantism* (Bloomington, Ind.: Indiana University Press, 1995), 71; Clarke, *Ten Great Religions: An Essay in Comparative Theology* (Boston: James R. Osgood and Co., 1871); Müller,

Introduction to the Science of Religion: Four Lectures Delivered at the Royal Institution (London: Longmans, Green, 1873), ix; Alger, *A Critical History of the Doctrine of a Future Life, with a Complete Bibliography of the Subject* [compiled by Ezra Abbot], 4th ed. (1860; New York: W. J. Widdleton, 1867); Clarke, *Ten Great Religions*, 3–4. On Alger, see Gary Scharnhorst, *A Literary Biography of William Rounseville Alger (1822–1905): A Neglected Member of the Concord Circle* (Lewiston, N.Y.: Edwin Mellen Press, 1990).

29. Clarke, *Ten Great Religions*, 1, 9.

30. Clarke, *Ten Great Religions*, part 2, *A Comparison of All Religions* (Boston: Houghton, Mifflin and Co., 1883), quotations at vi, vii.

31. Clarke, *Ten Great Religions*, unpaginated preface. I date publication in spring from Harvard's copy, which has "The Gift of the Publishers, May 1871" written on the library bookplate.

32. Samuel Johnson, *Oriental Religions and Their Relation to Universal Religion: India* (Boston: James R. Osgood and Co., 1872), followed Clarke's book by only a year and from the same publisher. The second volume, subtitled *China*, followed in 1877, and the last, *Persia*, posthumously in 1884. Like Clarke, Johnson popularized European scholarship rather than attempted original scholarship. Jackson, *Oriental Religions*, summarizes Johnson's work and career at 129–34.

33. Clarke, *Ten Great Religions*, preface, 3–4.

34. Clarke, *Ten Great Religions*, 2 (my emphasis).

35. Clarke, *Ten Great Religions*, 6, 7, 29, 139.

36. Clarke, *Ten Great Religions*, 6, 7, 15–17, 20, 29. In the internal 1865 Unitarian disputes that led to the forming of the Free Religious Association in 1867, Clarke sided with the more conservative Unitarians who affirmed Jesus Christ as Lord. Jackson, *Oriental Religions*, 123–24.

37. Georgina Max Müller, *The Life and Letters of the Right Honourable Friedrich Max Müller*, 2 vols. (London: Longmans, Green, and Co., 1902), 1: 483, 2: 1–2, 6–12, 35, 67, 282, 374; Nirad C. Chaudhuri, *Scholar Extraordinary: The Life of Professor the Rt. Hon. Friedrich Max Müller, P.C.* (New York: Oxford University Press, 1974), 348–56.

38. Louis Henry Jordan, *Comparative Religion: Its Genesis and Growth* (Edinburgh: T. & T. Clark, 1905); Hans G. Kippenberg, *Discovering Religious History in the Modern Age*, trans. Barbara Harshaw (1997; Princeton: Princeton University Press, 2002), chap. 4; Jacques Béguin et al., *Cents ans de sciences religieuses en France* (Paris: Cerf, 1987), 24; Crawford Howell Toy, *Introduction to the History of Religions* (Boston: Ginn and Co., 1913), vii; William Robertson Smith, *Religion of the Semites* (1894; New Brunswick, N.J.: Transaction Publishers, 2002), 17–18 (this 1894 second edition, enlarged and modified by Smith shortly before his death in the same year, is now taken as the standard text). My comment about Frazer draws on the draft chapter on comparative religion in my history of humanistic scholarship now in progress.

39. James Turner, "From Philology to Religion in Victorian Britain: The Cases of Friedrich Max Müller and William Robertson Smith," *Calcutta Historical Journal* 27, no. 2 (July–December 2007): 1–15.

40. [Salisbury?], "Buddhism," 182.

41. The quotation is from an English work also published and well known in the United States: Charles Hardwick, *Christ and Other Masters: An Historical Inquiry into Some of the Chief Parallelisms and Contrasts between Christianity and the Religious Systems of the Ancient World, with Special Reference to Prevailing Difficulties and Objections* (1855–59; London: Macmillan and Co., 1874), xii.

42. Robert A. Schneider, "Barrows, John Henry," *American National Biography*.

CHAPTER THREE. William James Redraws the Map

1. E.g., Hannah Adams had a long afterlife. *The Illustrated Book of All Religions from the Earliest Ages to the Present Time* (Philadelphia: John E. Potter & Co., 1893), very Christian-oriented, ripped off Adams's compilation.

2. But see James Turner, "Philology and the Generation of New Disciplines, 1825–1900," unpublished paper, Library of Congress, March 31, 2002.

3. See, e.g., the survey by Harvard's Crawford Howell Toy: C. H. Toy, "Recent Work in the Science of Religion," *International Monthly* 1 (1900): 217–34.

4. The most convenient source of information about early programs in comparative religion in American academe is Robert S. Shepard, *God's People in the Ivory Tower: Religion in the Early American University* (New York: Carlson Publishing, 1991). Lack of context hobbles Shepard's otherwise useful study. In his account, *Religionswissenschaft* in Europe springs from the brow of Max Müller, without ancestors, and then is simply imported into the United States. Shepard likewise slights the American non-academic antecedents of university-based religious studies; he ignores, e.g., the specifically Christian motives of James Freeman Clarke and slides over the Transcendentalist background that shaped his outlook in three words (Shepard, *God's People*, 78).

5. James C[lement]. Moffat, D.D., *A Comparative History of Religions*, part 1, *Ancient Scriptures* (New York: Dodd, Mead & Co., 1871), quotation at vi. A second volume appeared in 1873. For Moffat's 1852 comments on "Hindooism" see pages 32–33 above; for biographical data see the memorial sermon by his Princeton Theological Seminary colleague William Henry Green: *In Memoriam: James Clement Moffat, D.D., June 7, 1890* (Princeton, N.J.: n.p., 1890).

6. Shepard, *God's People*, 11–13.

7. Carl T. Jackson, *The Oriental Religions and American Thought: Nineteenth-Century Explorations* (Westport, Conn.: Greenwood Press, 1981), 124; Shepard, *God's People*, 80–87; Samuel A. Meier, "Moore, George Foot," *American National Biography*.

8. Brendan A. Rapple, "Warren, William Fairfield," *American National Biography*; Shepard, *God's People*, 11–13, 20–21, 24–31; Louis Henry Jordan, *Comparative Religion: Its Genesis and Growth* (Edinburgh: T. & T. Clark, 1905), 389; *New York Times*, May 15, 1894, p. 4, and December 17, 1899, p. 19; Frank F. Ellinwood, *Oriental Religions and Christianity* [the 1891 Ely Lectures] (New York: Charles Scribner's Sons, 1892). Tyler was promoted by Henry W. Sage, the wealthy philanthropist who endowed the school in which he taught.

9. William R. Harper, *The Report of the President: Publications of the Members of the University* (Chicago: University of Chicago Press, 1904), 38–39; "George Stephen Goodspeed," *Biblical World* 25 (1905): 169–72; Joseph M. Kitagawa, introduction to Joachim Wach, *Essays in the History of Religions* (New York: Macmillan Publishing Company, 1988), online edition (http://www.religion-online.org/showchapter. asp?title=578&C=744, accessed September 17, 2009).

10. Shepard, *God's People*, 32–38; Harold S. Wechsler, "Jastrow, Morris," *American National Biography*. For institutional context, see Bruce Kuklick, *Puritans in Babylon: The Ancient Near East and American Intellectual Life, 1880–1930* (Princeton: Princeton University Press, 1996), despite the expansive title essentially a study of the University of Pennsylvania (and not to be relied on for technical details of Assyriology).

11. "East Indian Faiths," *New York Times*, August 25, 1895, p. 23 (review of the first volume in the series, Edward Washburn Hopkins, *The Religions of India*).

12. Franklin Edgerton, "Edward Washburn Hopkins, 1857–1932," *Journal of the American Oriental Society* 52 (1932): 311–15; Jackson, *Oriental Religions*, 189–90.

13. Paul C. Wilt, "Kellogg, Samuel Henry," *American National Biography*; David G. Lyon, "Crawford Howell Toy," *Harvard Theological Review* 13 (1920): 1–22; Meier, "Moore,"; Shepard, *God's People*, 90; Morris Jastrow Jr., *The Study of Religion* (London: Walter Scott Publishing Co., 1911) (a book dedicated to Tiele); Walter H. Capps, *Religious Studies: The Making of a Discipline* (Minneapolis: Fortress Press, 1995), 122–24; quotation is from Wechsler, "Jastrow."

14. Jordan describes himself on the title page of his *Comparative Religion* as "Late Special Lecturer in Comparative Religion at the University of Chicago." According to the only biography I can find, Jordan resigned a pastorate in Montreal in 1890 "to undertake studies abroad in Comparative Religion" and then served as pastor of another Presbyterian church in Toronto from 1894 to 1900 before moving permanently to London. (See the brief biographies of ministers of the Erskine Presbyterian Church of Montreal: http://www.rootsweb.ancestry.com/~qcmtl-w/

ErskineMinisters.html, accessed September 17, 2009.) This sequence would put Jordan in Chicago in the earliest years of the comparative religion program there. I get his dates from the record of a library bequest he left to the School of Oriental and African Studies of the University of London: http://www.ucl.ac.uk/ls/masc25/full.php?CollectionID=190 (accessed April 1, 2010).

15. "Goodspeed," *Biblical World*; Caroline E. Haskell to William Rainey Harper, May 5 and October 12, 1894, quoted in Thomas Wakefield Goodspeed, *A History of the University of Chicago, Founded by John D. Rockefeller: The First Quarter Century* (Chicago: University of Chicago Press, 1916), 323; Goodspeed, *University of Chicago*, 323; Jordan, *Comparative Religion*, 594; John Henry Barrows, *Christianity, the World Religion* (Chicago: A. C. McClurg and Company, 1897); idem., *The Christian Conquest of Asia: Studies and Personal Observations of Oriental Religions* (New York: Charles Scribner's Sons, 1899).

16. Samuel H. Kellogg, *Handbook of Comparative Religion* (Philadelphia: Westminster Press, 1915); Levi Leonard Paine, *The Ethnic Trinities and Their Relations to the Christian Trinity: A Chapter in the Comparative History of Religions* (Boston: Houghton, Mifflin & Co., 1901), [v], vii; Shepard, *God's People*, 38–39.

17. The term appears in 1885 in C. P. T[iele], "Religions," *Encyclopædia Britannica*, 9th ed. (1885; New York: Henry G. Allen Co., 1890), 20: 367. Tiele used it to label religions "which start from principles and maxims." Religions "founded on a law or sacred writing" he called "nomistic." Tomoko Masuzawa, *The Invention of World Religions; or, How European Universalism was Preserved in the Language of Pluralism* (Chicago: University of Chicago Press, 2005), 109, says this was the first usage of the phrase in English.

18. Toy, "Recent Work," 221, 225 (my emphasis).

19. George Foot Moore, *History of Religions* (New York: Charles Scribner's Sons, 1913), viii. For Sharpe's claim, see page 6 above.

20. Crawford Howell Toy, *Introduction to the History of Religions* (Boston: Ginn and Co., 1913), may seem to contradict this claim, since it attended perhaps more often to 'primitive' religions than to 'higher'

ones. But Toy's book was written as the introductory volume in the series Handbooks on the History of Religions mentioned earlier (edited by Morris Jastrow), in which individual volumes by different authors were to cover 'higher' religious traditions.

21. Kellogg, *Handbook*, iii.

22. Moore, *History of Religions*, v (my emphasis). 'Comparative theology' was used in Europe; e.g., C. P. T[iele], "Religions," 20: 358. The difference is that Tiele used it to label one subsection of the study of religions; Clarke used it as the general term.

23. *The Varieties of Religious Experience: A Study in Human Nature, Being the Gifford Lectures on Natural Religion Delivered at Edinburgh in 1901–02* (London, New York, and Bombay: Longmans, Green, and Co., 1902); quotation at [v]. The copyright page of the text I use gives the date of the first edition as June 1902; my copy was "Reprinted, with revisions, August, 1902." The literature on James is vast. I cite below only works that have influenced my understanding on specific points in this study.

24. James, *Varieties*, 80.

25. David Hume, *Four Dissertations. I. The Natural History of Religion. II. Of the Passions. III. Of Tragedy. IV. Of the Standard of Taste* (London: Printed for A. Millar, 1757), 13; Publius Papinius Statius, *The Thebaid*, 3: 661 (I quote the old J. H. Mozley Loeb Library translation, available online at http://www.theoi.com/Text/StatiusThebaid1.html, accessed January 21, 2010); Friedrich Schleiermacher, *Der christliche Glaube nach den Grundsätzen der evangelischen Kirche in Zusammenhange dargestellt*, 2 vols. (Berlin: G. Reimer, 1821–22); William Robertson Smith, *[Lectures on the] Religion of the Semites* (1894; New Brunswick, N.J.: Transaction, 2002) 57–59 (lecture 2); Jastrow, *Study of Religion*, 280–81; Toy, "Recent Work," 224; Toy, *Introduction*, 2–4.

26. I aim only to position the New Psychology with respect to comparative religion as then practiced in the United States and to sketch James's attitude toward New Psychological study of religion as he set about writing *Varieties*. Readers who want a fuller discussion should refer to Ann Taves, *Fits, Trances, and Visions: Experiencing Religion and Explaining Experience from Wesley to James* (Princeton: Princeton University Press, 1999), chap.

7 — a subtle, well informed discussion of the New Psychology's treatment of religion.

27. James H. Leuba, "A Study in the Psychology of Religious Phenomena," *American Journal of Psychology* 7 (1896): 309–85; Edwin Diller Starbuck, "A Study of Conversion," *American Journal of Psychology* 8 (1897): 268–308; idem, "Contributions to the Psychology of Religion," *American Journal of Psychology* 9 (1897): 70–124; cf. Leuba, *Studies in the Psychology of Religious Phenomena: The Religious Motive, Conversion, Facts, and Doctrines* (Worcester, Mass.: Orpha, 1896); Starbuck, *The Psychology of Religion: An Empirical Study of the Growth of Religious Consciousness* (London: Walter Scott Publishing Co., 1899); David Arnold, "Starbuck, Edwin Diller," *American National Biography*; Jon H. Roberts, "James H. Leuba," in *Dictionary of Modern American Philosophers*, ed. John R. Shook, 4 vols. (Bristol: Thoemmes, 2005), 3: 1446–47. Arthur H. Daniels, "The New Life: A Study of Regeneration," *American Journal of Psychology* 6 (1893): 61–106, appears from its title to represent an earlier instance of such work; it is in fact a jumble of anthropology and unsystematic psychologizing.

28. William James, preface to Starbuck, *Psychology*; Taves, *Fits, Trances, and Visions*, 264–66; George A. Coe, *The Spiritual Life: Studies in the Science of Religion* (New York: Eaton & Mains, Cincinnati: Jennings & Pye, 1900); David M. Wulff, "Coe, George Albert," *American National Biography*; Ian Nicholson, "Academic Professionalization and Protestant Reconstruction, 1890–1902: George Albert Coe's Psychology of Religion," *Journal of the History of the Behavioral Sciences* 30 (1994): 348–68; Hendrika Vande Kemp, "G. Stanley Hall and the Clark School of Religious Psychology," *American Psychologist* 47 (1992): 290–98.

29. See the survey in Louis Henry Jordan, *Comparative Religion: Its Adjuncts and Allies* (London: Oxford University Press, 1915), 136–62.

30. Shepard, *God's People*, 80–83; Ephraim Emerton, "Charles Carroll Everett," *Proceedings of the American Academy of Arts and Sciences* 36 (1900–1901): 549–52; "Charles Carroll Everett (1829–1900)," in *Harvard Divinity School at the Turn of the Last Century*, http://www.hds.harvard. edu/library/exhibits/online/hdsturncentury/everett.html (accessed

January 26, 2010); William W. Fenn, "The Theology of Charles Carroll Everett," *Harvard Theological Review* 3 (1910): 1–23; Charles Carroll Everett, *The Science of Thought*, rev. ed. (1869; Boston: De Wolfe, Fiske & Co., 1890); Everett, *Religions before Christianity* (Boston: Unitarian Sunday-School Society, 1883). Quotation from "Everett (1829–1900)." I have not seen the first edition of the book that landed Everett his Harvard job.

31. C. H. Toy, preface to Charles Carroll Everett, *The Psychological Elements of Religious Faith: Lectures*, ed. Edward Hale (New York: Macmillan Company, 1902), vi; Edward Hale, editor's preface, ibid., vii; Richard Crouter, "Hegel and Schleiermacher at Berlin: A Many-Sided Debate," *Journal of the American Academy of Religion* 48 (1980): 19–43; Everett, *Psychological Elements*, 18, 130–31. In his lectures on theology proper, Everett went in a more explicitly Hegelian direction: Everett, *Theism and the Christian Faith: Lectures Delivered in the Harvard Divinity School*, ed. Edward Hale (New York: Macmillan Company, 1909).

32. Ralph Barton Perry, *The Thought and Character of William James*, 2 vols. (Boston: Little, Brown and Co., 1935), 1: 712–13, 2: 463; William James to Charles W. Eliot, December 24, 1900, and James to Frances R. Morse, August [error: July] 10, 1901, in *The Correspondence of William James*, ed. Ignas K. Skrupskelis and Elizabeth M. Berkeley, 12 vols. (Charlottesville: University Press of Virginia, 1992–2004), 9: 391, 528.

33. My summary of James's life and religious background relies on Perry, *Thought and Character*; Gay Wilson Allen, *William James: A Biography* (New York: Viking Press, 1967); Gerald E. Myers, *William James: His Life and Thought* (New Haven: Yale University Press, 1986); Paul Jerome Croce, *Science and Religion in the Era of William James: Eclipse of Certainty, 1820–1880* (Chapel Hill: University of North Carolina Press, 1995); Robert D. Richardson, *William James: In the Maelstrom of American Modernism: A Biography* (Boston: Houghton Mifflin Co., 2006). See also the acute biographical comments in Paul Croce, "Nature's Beloved Incarnations: Inquiry, Conviction, and William James," *American Journal of Theology and Philosophy* 30 (2009): 303–7. I do not find very plausible another

well-known study, Howard M. Feinstein, *Becoming William James* (Ithaca: Cornell University Press, 1984).

34. James, *Varieties*, 160–61; Perry, *Thought and Character*, 1: 322; Paul J. Croce, "A Mannered Memory and Teachable Moment: William James and the French Correspondent in the *Varieties*," *William James Studies* 4 (2009): 54; Myers, *James*, 468, 477. Croce, "Mannered Memory," 36–50, magisterially surveys the very many interpretations and datings of this episode and of James's depression and its consequences more generally.

35. Palmer quoted in Croce, *Science and Religion*, 229; Holmes to Frederick Pollock, September 1, 1910, in Mark DeWolfe Howe, ed., *Holmes-Pollock Letters: The Correspondence of Mr. Justice Holmes and Sir Frederick Pollock, 1874–1932*, 2 vols. (Cambridge, Mass.: Harvard University Press, 1941), 1: 167. I thank David Hollinger for Holmes's bon mot; Holmes was referring specifically to James's half-belief in spiritualism (psychic research). On agnosticism in this period, see James Turner, *Without God, Without Creed: The Origins of Unbelief in America* (Baltimore: Johns Hopkins University Press, 1985), part 2.

36. James, *Varieties*, 519; James, *The Will to Believe and Other Essays in Popular Philosophy* (1897; New York: Longmans, Green, and Co., 1912), 1.

37. Wayne Proudfoot, ed., *William James and a Science of Religions: Reexperiencing "The Varieties of Religious Experience"* (New York: Columbia University Press, 2004), 2, is only one of the more recent works to stress how pragmatism shaped *Varieties*.

38. James, *Varieties*, 2.

39. Croce, "Nature's Beloved Incarnations," 307.

40. Coe, *Spiritual Life*, 5.

41. William James, *The Principles of Psychology* (1890; Cambridge, Mass.: Harvard University Press, 1983), chap. 9, esp. 273–77. Although the chapter title is "The Stream of Thought," James also used within it the phrase "stream of consciousness."

42. On the importance in *Varieties* of a subconscious self, subliminal consciousness, or what James called an "extra-marginal self" (*Varieties*, 518), see Ann Taves, "The Fragmentation of Consciousness and *The*

Varieties of Religious Experience: William James's Contribution to a Theory of Religion," in Proudfoot, ed., *James and Science of Religions*, 48–72.

43. Richardson, *James*, 95; James, *Varieties*, 2–3.

44. James, *Varieties*, 431–33, 436–39, 456.

45. *American Journal of Religious Psychology and Education* 1 (1904–05): title page. WorldCat entries show that the journal sank in 1915 or 1916.

46. Its original title was the Association of Biblical Instructors in American Colleges and Secondary Schools. The name changed to National Association of Biblical Instructors in 1922.

47. Proudfoot, *Religious Experience* (Berkeley: University of California Press, 1985); Rabinowitz, *The Spiritual Self in Everyday Life: The Transformation of Personal Religious Experience in Nineteenth-Century New England* (Boston: Northeastern University Press, 1989); for Taves, see note 26 above. Proudfoot's statement as recently as 2003 that scholars have "neglected" *Varieties* is puzzling. (Proudfoot, ed., *James and Science of Religions*, 1; I assume Proudfoot, as editor, wrote the unsigned introduction.) Perhaps his view reflects his perspective as someone focused on religious experience in a discipline where the great majority of scholars do take different approaches.

INDEX

〰〰〰〰〰〰〰〰〰〰〰〰〰〰〰

Except for four works discussed at length in this book and indexed under their titles, references to written works are indexed under authors, without titles. References to religious texts, such as the Qur'an and the Vedas, are indexed as the faiths with which they are associated, except for the Bible. References to any version of Christianity except Unitarianism will be found under 'Christianity.' (The author disclaims a soft spot for the Bible or Unitarians, but he needs to mention both frequently.) References to religions of specific tribal peoples are grouped as 'tribal religions,' those to specific ancient Mediterranean religions as 'paganism.'

CPSIA information can be obtained
at www.ICGtesting.com
Printed in the USA
LVHW111936150119
604022LV00005B/453/P

9 780820 344188